P9-DDY-878

The Glory of the Ministry

Paul's Exultation in Preaching

by

A. T. Robertson

Introduction by

Ralph G. Turnbull

BAKER BOOK HOUSE
Grand Rapids, Michigan

Library of Congress Catalog Card Number: 67-18193

Reprinted 1967 by
Baker Book House Company
from the original printing
made in 1911 by
Fleming H. Revell Company

PHOTOLITHOPRINTED BY CUSHING - MALLOY, INC.
ANN ARBOR, MICHIGAN, UNITED STATES OF AMERICA
1967

Notable Books on Preaching

Among the helps for the minister and the theological student are the many volumes on preaching and homiletics. On our shelves are the single volumes written by individual men. There are well known series of lectures, such as the Yale or Lyman Beecher given at Yale Divinity School, New Haven, and the Warrack given to the four University Theological colleges in Scotland. Not many today possess full sets of these famous lectures. Earlier works are unobtainable as they are out of print and some cease to appeal. Nevertheless, the preacher who has access to this thesaurus of preaching and homiletics finds much to suggest and stimulate. Because of this, the time is opportune to select and reissue some of the books which have stood the test of time and have proved of abiding value.

It is proposed to issue a selection over the next few years. Not all will be alike. The homiletical techniques will be observed in them, but the emphases will vary. The wisdom and experience of those who have labored in other days may prove of lasting value in many a difficult hour. The particular books have been chosen in the belief that each will minister to the preacher in different moods of the soul. Representative of those which will be selected are:

The Public Worship of God, by J. R. P. Sclater (Worship)

In Christ's Stead, by A. J. Gossip (Ambassador)

The Building of the Church, by C. E. Jefferson (Church)

The Preacher and his Models, by J. Stalker (Isa. & Paul)

Puritan Preaching in England, by J. Brown (Puritan)

God's Word through Preaching, by J. Hall (Bible)

The Romance of Preaching, by C. S. Horne (History)

The Cure of Souls, by J. Watson (Pastoral)

The Glory of the Ministry, by A. T. Robertson (Exegetical)

Good Ministers of Jesus Christ, by W. F. McDowell (Devotional)

"Preaching can never lose its place so long as the mystery and wonder of the human spirit remain" is the judgment of Charles Sylvester Horne, *The Romance of Preaching*. Believing in the supremacy of preaching as God-appointed for the Church, the minister must equip himself for an incredible task of service. One of the causes of failure in the ministry lies in the lack of definite reading and study. These books will serve to spur on the preacher to greater deeds. We need not copy any man, but we can learn from all who have blazed the trail before us. "Who keeps one end in view, Makes all things serve" (R. Browning).

In issuing these volumes it is our hope and prayer that they will help to keep the ideals fresh and the standards from sagging while the vision remains clear. We must "plod on and keep the passion fresh."

RALPH G. TURNBULL

The First Presbyterian Church
of Seattle, Washington

Introduction

Archibald Thomas Robertson (1864-1934)
The Glory of the Ministry

Robertson served as Professor of New Testament Interpretation in The Southern Baptist Theological Seminary, Louisville, Kentucky, from 1888 to 1934. He trained hundreds of students in the use of the Greek language. His voluminous work, *A Grammar of the Greek New Testament in the Light of Historical Research,* is an indispensable tool for the graduate student. The denomination and the seminary had John A. Broadus with his *On the Preparation and Delivery of Sermons* and his inspiring preaching, but Robertson was the more popular interpreter of the New Testament by his lectures and teaching in conferences. This volume is a sample.

The book deals with "Paul's Exultation in Preaching" and is an exegetical and expository treatise of 2 Corinthians 2:12 – 6:10. Given first in class room to students it was then shared with ministers and the public. The interpretation is geared to human needs and is no academic recital of the text. The professor kindles the fire for the preacher. Formal homiletics is not obvious, but the professor's enthusiasm in the use of the Greek text is catching. Robertson's theory of preaching is to take the original and exegete it in context and then interpret for today. The study must precede the work of the pulpit.

The thesis of this book is "how can men expect to preach from the Bible unless they know it intimately?" Thus exegesis and exposition lie at the heart of Biblical preaching. This is a seminal book and its message may well stab afresh the homiletical conscience in this lethargic age.

RALPH G. TURNBULL

Preface

IT is now a good many years since the beauty of Paul's apologetic for preaching in 2 Corinthians ii. 12–vi. 10 made its first appeal to me. As with much that has entered my life, it was the close study of the Greek text with a class in Greek exegesis that first gripped my heart with this noble panegyric on the ministry of the servants of Jesus Christ. It is not mere rhapsody on Paul's part, but a magnificent exposition of the preacher's task from every point of view. I have made it my duty and joy to present this lofty spiritual interpretation of the minster's work to succeeding classes of theological students. Last November in South Carolina I made an address on "The Glory of the Ministry" as presented by Paul in this passage. It brought cheer and hope to the hearts of some of the toilers for Christ to the extent that a number of them privately asked me to write a little book on the subject. I have not been able to get away from this appeal. My life is constantly with ministers. I know much of the struggles, ambitions, hopes, joys, and disappointments of preachers of the Gospel, both young and old. The lines have not fallen in pleasant places for all of them. They are subject to much misunderstanding. Modern and public opinion is distinctly critical, if not at times harsh, towards the minister. It is not always easy in an unsympathetic atmosphere to preserve the right spirit and to see things as they really are. I have written this book out of love for preachers of the Gospel of Jesus. Some one may find tonic and ozone, as he comes close to the heart of his mission and life, in Paul's bracing words. Some, for whom the ministry no longer has the old charm, may recover their first love. Some, who have been disposed to speak unkindly of ministers as a class, may be led to revise their judgment. Some young men, who look out on the wonderful modern world, may catch a glimpse of the light in the face of Jesus, as did Paul on the road to Damascus, and yield to the appeal in that Face for a world lost in sin, a world that calls for interpreters of Jesus. I pray that the Spirit of Christ may go with this little book and take it where it is needed. The volume is not a mere exposition of Paul's own glorying in the ministry, though that is the heart of it. Paul's grand conception is related to modern ideas of the ministry by sufficient use of the great writers of our time on the preacher's problems. These are shown to share Paul's enthusiasm. The flame of the Lord that burned in Paul's breast blazes yet. Many of the noblest spirits of our time answer the call of Christ with joy and gladness of heart.

The substance of this book was delivered in addresses before the Tabernacle Bible Conference (Atlanta, Ga., March, 1911), but the book has been written independently of that occasion.

A. T. ROBERTSON.

Louisville, Ky.

Contents

I

THE DISHEARTENED PREACHER'S JOY —THE NEW STANDPOINT

(*2 Cor. ii. 12–iii. 6*)

> "I had no relief for my spirit . . .
> But thanks be unto God, who always leadeth us in triumph in Christ."
>
> —*2 Cor. ii. 13 f.*

I

THE DISHEARTENED PREACHER'S JOY—THE NEW STANDPOINT

1. *The Ground of Paul's Discouragement*

IT was chiefly the situation in Corinth, a church that Paul had founded.[1] He loved this church very greatly. It seemed to have the greatest opportunity for usefulness and power of any of the European churches. It was in a new atmosphere of wealth and progress. The city had been restored by Julius Cæsar after being in ruins for a hundred years since Mummius destroyed it. It was more open to the Gospel than Athens where a fondness for philosophical speculation made it hard to win a foothold.[2] Corinth had been more fertile ground. Indeed, Paul had succeeded only too well there, for the Jews soon grew jealous of his power.[3] Two years[4] Paul had lived and laboured in this great and wicked metropolis. It had not been in vain. He had seen the ruler of the Jewish synagogue, Crispus, become a Christian.[5] He had received from Gallio,

[1] Acts xviii. 1–20. [2] Acts xvii. 16–34. [3] Acts xviii. 5–17.
[4] Acts xviii. 11, 18. [5] Acts xviii. 7f.

the new proconsul, the first official permission to preach the Gospel in the Roman Empire that gave Christianity a new standing in the Province of Achaia.[1] Paul loved the church in Corinth with his whole heart. "For though ye have ten thousand tutors in Christ, yet have ye not many fathers; for in Christ Jesus I begat you through the Gospel."[2] But a series of mishaps had come to the work in Corinth. One disaster had followed another till Paul feared the very worst. Few sadder experiences come to the preacher than to see the work of his heart crumble away after he has left it. Almost all of the modern preacher's difficulties confronted Paul in the work at Corinth. He could not shake off "that which presseth upon me daily, anxiety for all the churches."[3] The pressure[4] was like a nightmare that weighed upon him unceasingly. The anxiety[5] ate into his soul like corroding rust. Paul knew how to preach: "In nothing be anxious."[6] But it is easier to preach than to practice. No church pressed upon Paul's heart quite so heavily as did

[1] Ramsay, "St. Paul the Traveller," pp. 257 f.; Robertson, "Epochs in the Life of Paul," pp. 165 f.; Acts xviii. 12–17.

[2] 1 Cor. iv. 15.

[3] 2 Cor. xi. 28 ἡ ἐπίστασίς μοι ἡ καθ' ἡμέραν, ἡ μέριμνα πασῶν τῶν ἐκκλησιῶν.

[4] ἐπί-στασις standing upon.

[5] μέριμνα.

[6] Phil. iv. 6 μηδὲν μεριμνᾶτε. Present imperative with μή implies that they were anxious. "Quit being anxious."

that in Corinth. It was a richly endowed church with great spiritual gifts and possibilities.[1] But these very endowments of grace had become the occasion of envy and faction. The divisions showed themselves even at the Lord's Supper in unseemly scramble and selfishness.[2] They would not even wait for one another. There was schism in the body of Christ and the members were hostile towards one another.[3] The very services in church were scenes of disorder and confusion.[4] They took sides for Paul and against Paul, for Apollos and against Apollos, for Cephas and against Cephas.[5] It was so bad that Apollos would not stay nor would he return to Corinth, though Paul urged him.[6] Some praised the oratory of Apollos, others probably thought him too "flowery." Some thought that Paul's speech was of no account,[7] while others stoutly defended Paul as the founder of the Church and the gifted Apostle of the Gentiles. The household of Chloe[8] in particular reported to Paul in Ephesus the sad situation. Peter had probably not been to Corinth, but there had been a momentary breach between Paul and Peter at Antioch over the question of social affiliation with

[1] 1 Cor. i. 4–9, 12–14.
[2] 1 Cor. xi. 18 ff., 33.
[3] 1 Cor. xii. 25.
[4] 1 Cor. xiv.
[5] 1 Cor. i. 10–13; iii. 21 ff.; iv. 6 ff.
[6] Acts xviii. 27–xix. 1; 1 Cor. xvi. 12.
[7] 2 Cor. x. 10.
[8] 1 Cor. iv. 11.

the Gentile Christians,[1] and the Judaizers had been swift to make the most of it and had claimed Peter as on their side in the controversy with Paul. As a matter of fact Peter was really with Paul and he had shown merely momentary weakness when the Judaizers, under the unwarranted use of the name of James, refused to recognize the Gentiles as Christians unless they became Jews also. These Judaizers had been silenced for the moment at the Jerusalem conference,[2] but had reopened the controversy on a more extensive scale than before. They had come to Corinth and had used the name of Peter in support of their campaign against Paul. There was also a partisan use of the name of Christ by one faction in the Church. Doctrinal issues thus became mixed with intense personalities and jealousies. Few modern churches have had a more deplorable schism than was a reality in Corinth. Besides, gross immorality was winked at by the majority.[3] The feeling was so intense that the members would go to law against one another before heathen judges.[4] There were abuses concerning marriage.[5] There was a breach between the enlightened and the unenlightened elements of the Church on the subject of meats offered to idols.[6] The liberal and the reactionary

[1] Acts xv. 1–35; Gal. ii. [2] Acts xv. 1–30; Gal. ii. 1–10.
[3] 1 Cor. v. [4] 1 Cor. vi. 1–11. [5] 1 Cor. vii. [6] 1 Cor. viii.–x.

parties were at daggers' points with each other. Some of them had gone so far in doctrinal error as to deny the resurrection.[1] The collection for the poor saints in Jerusalem, which Paul had pushed with energy elsewhere, had sadly fallen behind in Corinth,[2] and no wonder, with all the strife and confusion rampant there. It was enough to break any preacher's heart. Paul rose to the occasion grandly. He wrote them a letter which is lost to us.[3] Then he sent Timothy, his beloved son in the gospel, to see what he could do.[4] Timothy, though warmly commended to the Church,[5] seems not to have been very successful in his mission. It is possible that Timothy was mistreated in Corinth because Paul himself was expected.[6] Paul had indeed intended to go to Corinth, but had meanwhile sent Timothy. He hoped to come soon, but did not wish to come with a rod.[7] He did later speak of a "third time,"[8] but this is probably intention, not fact. Indeed the situation was so bad that Paul did not wish to go to Corinth. He must needs come with sorrow in that case.[9] He remained away on purpose and allowed

[1] 1 Cor. xv. [2] 1 Cor. xvi. 1 f.; 2 Cor. viii. and ix.
[3] 1 Cor. v. 9, 11. [4] 1 Cor. iv. 17. [5] 1 Cor. xvi. 10.
[6] Cf. Findlay, "Paul" in Hastings's B. D.; Robertson, "Epochs in the Life of Paul," p. 191.
[7] 1 Cor. iv. 17–21. [8] 2 Cor. xii. 14; xiii. 1.
[9] 2 Cor. i. 15, 23; ii. 1; xii. 21.

himself to be charged with fickleness[1] and cowardice[2] rather than come while his indignation was at such heat. Meanwhile, the Church sent a special deputation (Stephanus, Fortunatus, Achaicus)[3] to Paul. Paul wrote the powerful Epistle called First Corinthians in which he poured out his heart to them. After the return of Timothy Paul sent Titus, who seemed to be made of sterner stuff than Timothy. It is possible that Paul sent another letter with Titus, demanding an apology for the treatment of Timothy. If so, that letter is lost to us.[4] The plan was for Titus to come back *via* Macedonia and meet Paul at Troas.[5] Paul was to leave Ephesus about Pentecost for Corinth through Macedonia.[6] At Troas he would thus meet Titus and learn how things went in Corinth.

But our best laid plans "aft gang agley." Paul seems to have had a well-nigh fatal sickness in Ephesus soon after writing First Corinthians. "We ourselves have had the sentence of death within ourselves."[7] Death came so close to Paul that he seemed to get the "answer"[8] in speech. The peril

[1] 2 Cor. i. 15–20. [2] 2 Cor. x. 8–11. [3] 1 Cor. xvi. 17.

[4] Some scholars hold that 2 Corinthians x.–xiii. is this lost letter which has been put in the wrong place in 2 Corinthians. I do not accept that view. See Robertson, "Epochs in the Life of Paul," p. 196.

[5] 2 Cor. ii. 12 f.; vii. 5–7. [6] 1 Cor. xvi. 5–8.

[7] 2 Cor. i. 9. [8] The "sentence."

was so great that it is still a vivid reality to Paul as he writes.[1] So he seemed to be dying.[2] Thus it was out of his experience that Paul could write so sympathetically about death.[3] In his great physical weakness the daily duties of life were a burden to him, not to mention the serious situation in Corinth. His weakened nerves would make the troubles seem magnified a hundredfold.

But this was not all. While Paul was in this overwrought state a riot occurred in Ephesus. Demetrius had organized the silversmiths into a mob against Paul. The whole city was soon in an uproar in the theatre.[4] Paul, probably because of his sickness, was not found, though his companions in travel, Gaius and Aristarchus, were seized. Paul could with difficulty be restrained from rushing into the theatre. The Asiarchs helped the disciples restrain Paul.[5] So Paul's life was saved, but it was not prudent for him to remain in Ephesus. He left in rather short order for Macedonia.[6] Paul was somewhat like the preacher who has resigned without a call to another field. His departure from Ephesus was sudden and unceremonious, but he had the world before him. He was used to moving on when he was no longer welcome. Will he be more welcome in Corinth?

[1] Historical present perfect. [2] 2 Cor. vi. 9. [3] 2 Cor. iv. and v.
[4] Acts xix. 23–28. [5] Acts xix. 29–31. [6] Acts xx. 1.

2. *Paul's Restless Spirit at Troas*

He was apparently alone at Troas, for Timothy and Erastus had already been sent on to Macedonia.[1] It was not yet time for Titus to arrive at Troas. It was at Troas that Paul had met Luke and had received the call to go to Macedonia.[2] Then it had not been possible for Paul to do much work in Troas. Now in God's providence he is here again. Perhaps the hand of God is in it. He had come "for the gospel of Christ."[3] Paul had evidently looked forward to this opportunity to be a blessing to Troas. Besides, "a door was opened unto me in the Lord."[4] It was not a mere general situation, but apparently Paul means to say that direct appeals came to him to speak a word for Jesus. But it was of no use. "I had no relief for my spirit, because I found not Titus my brother."[5] It is a vivid reality to Paul now, as he writes, "I have not had any release for my spirit." The tension had become acute. It had gone on so long that it was chronic. He could not throw it off. In truth, he was incapacitated for work of any kind. He needed Luke, who was probably in Philippi, to take hold of him and bring him back to health. Many a preacher has found himself caught in the coil of circumstances, as was Paul, when he

[1] Acts xix. 29–41. [2] Acts xvi. 8–10. [3] 2 Cor. ii. 12.
[4] 2 Cor. ii. 12. [5] 2 Cor. ii. 13. Historical present perfect.

cannot respond to the calls for service that come to him, cannot enter the doors that open to him. This is a dangerous hour for the preacher. His heart is in danger of rebellion. Then when the door is closed, the door that opened to large fields of usefulness, resentment may harden the heart. There was no happiness for Paul in Troas. He had lost his zest for work and idleness was despair. He was more miserable alone than otherwise. He knew that it was not yet time for Titus to come, for Paul had come on ahead of time. But, none the less, his spirit chafed at the limitations of his plight. Everything seemed to have gone wrong. There was no joy any more for Paul's restless spirit. One of the charges made against some ministers to-day is just this restlessness of spirit here shown by Paul. One is seized with a feverish desire to go elsewhere, to get a call to a more hopeful field, to resign this field, to move on to pastures new. There comes a sense of drudgery in the tasks of every-day life. The gold is at the end of the rainbow, and here is only steady, plodding toil in a rather humdrum ministry. The temptation may even come to give up the ministry and enter some other calling. At such a time one is oversensitive and imagines all kinds of slights and insults. The real difficulties and problems of the ministry are magnified out of all proportion to the facts. In such a case a minister is in jeopardy. He is in danger of becoming bitter towards the world, jealous of other ministers, disgusted with his own task. Thus he will lose his compass and drift out to sea.

In *The Standard* (Chicago) for January 7, 1911, there is printed the following letter:

"MY DEAR JIM: I am through. Yesterday I handed in my resignation, to take effect at once, and this morning I began work for the ——— Land Company. I shall not return to the pastorate. I think I can see into your heart as you read these words and behold not a little disappointment, if not disgust. I don't blame you at all, for I am somewhat disgusted with myself. Do you recall the days in the seminary when we talked of the future and painted pictures of what we were to do for the kingdom of God? We saw the boundless need for unselfish Christian service and longed to be out among men doing our part towards the world's redemption. I shall never forget that last talk on the night before our graduation. You were to go to the foreign field and I to the First Church, of ———. We had brave dreams of usefulness, and you have realized them. As I look back across twenty-five years I can see some lives that I have helped, and some things which I have been permitted to do that are worth while; but, sitting here to-night, I am more than half convinced that God never intended me to be a minister. If He did, I am not big enough and brave enough to pay the price. Even if it leads you to write me down a coward, I'm going to tell you why I've quit.

"To be perfectly honest with you, money has had

much to do with my decision. I think you will not charge me with being mercenary in those days when you knew me well, and I am not conscious of caring any more for money now than I did then. I have never desired to be rich; I do not now desire to be. I have not gone into business with any expectation of making a fortune, but I do want to have something for the years when I can no longer work, and for my family, if I should be taken from them. I do want to be able to meet my bills as they fall due. A month ago in our ministers' meeting an old minister, shabby almost to raggedness, arose and told us that he and his wife were on the verge of starvation. He had no money, his credit was exhausted, they had no food, no coal, and were about to be put upon the street because they could not pay the rent. We raised some thirty dollars among us and gave it to him, and I suppose he will go to the home for aged ministers; but it scared me. I saw myself in him. What reason have I to expect that I shall not be where he is twenty years from now?

"Frugality? Well, I have not been thriftless. Wife and I have tried hard to lay by a little each year. We did get $500 saved up, and then Edna was taken with tuberculosis and it all went, and much more, before God took her home. I had $1,000 per year from the church at B——. They paid it promptly, and possibly some men would have been able to save something out of it each year. We tried our best, and failed. Once the church thought of increasing the pastor's salary, but Deacon Edmunds argued that the minister should trust God; said that when he began life he only had an income of $200 for the first year; spoke of the joys of Christian sacrifice; pointed to the Saviour of the world and His self-abnegation, and the salary was not increased. I may say that the deacon is supposed to be worth not less than $200,000. Then I was called to this field at $1,200 per year. I have been here seven years, and there has never been a month since the beginning when my salary has been paid promptly. At times the church has owed me $600 and $700. I have borrowed and paid interest, have 'stood off' my creditors until I was ashamed to go upon the street, have scrimped and twisted and wiggled until my soul was raw. I've had enough.

"Other things have contributed to my decision. In these years I have found not a few earnest, unselfish, consecrated Christians. I do not believe that I am specially morbid or unfair in my estimate. So far as I know my own heart, I am not bitter. But through all these years a conviction has been growing within me that the average church-member cares precious little about the kingdom of God and its advancement, or the welfare of his fellow men. He is a Christian in order that he may save his soul from hell, and for no other reason. He does as little as he can, lives as indifferently as he dares. If he thought he could gain heaven without even lifting his finger for others, he would jump at the chance. Never have I known more than a small minority of any church which I have served to be really interested in and unselfishly devoted to God's work. It took my whole time to pull and push and urge and persuade the reluctant members of my church to undertake a little something for their fellow men. They took a covenant to be faithful in attendance upon the services of the church, and not one out of ten ever thought of attending prayer-meeting. A large percentage seldom attended church in the morning, and a pitifully small number in the evening. It did not seem to mean anything to them that they had dedicated themselves to the service of Christ.

"I am tired; tired of being the only one in the

church from whom real sacrifice is expected; tired of straining and tugging to get Christian people to live like Christians; tired of planning work for my people and then being compelled to do it myself or see it left undone; tired of dodging my creditors when I would not need to if I had what is due me; tired of the affrighting vision of a penniless old age. I am not leaving Christ. I love Him. I shall still try to serve Him.

"Judge me leniently, old man, for I cannot bear to lose your friendship.

"Yours as of old,

"WILLIAM."

The editor vouches for the genuineness of this letter. It is probably an actual experience, an extreme instance of a broken-hearted preacher of to-day.

But a most notable instance of struggle and triumph is revealed in the "Early Letters of Marcus Dods." In his Diary for March 8, 1860, p. 382, we read this confession of his experience as a "probationer": "No day passes without strong temptation to give up this work—this temptation appeals to me on the ground that I am not fitted for pastoral work; writing sermons is often the hardest labour to me, visiting is terrible. I often stand before a door unable to ring or knock—sometimes I have gone away without entering. A lowness of spirit that it costs me a great deal to throw off is the consequence of this, and a real doubt whether it would not be better for myself and all whom it may concern that

I should at once look for some work that I could overtake. However, the one thing that has kept me going hitherto is this, that when I am in the best of spirit these disinclinations to work go from me, and I fear I have hitherto had so little comfort in the work only because my habitual state is unspiritual." He was, in fact, a probationer for six years, a really terrible experience for a young minister. But Marcus Dods came to be the principal of New College and one of the chief Biblical scholars and preachers of the world.

But it may be noticed that deep down as Paul had gone, it did not occur to him to quit the ministry. He was entitled to pay which he did not receive from the Church at Corinth.[1] He proved his right to receive a man's pay for his work, but he would not receive it from a church like that at Corinth which taunted him for not taking pay like a regular apostle.[2] He had seen days in Corinth when he "was in want," but he had kept his manhood and independence and "was not a burden on any man." He had even "robbed other churches, taking wages of them that I might minister unto you." He had made tents with Aquila and Priscilla so as to get a living while he preached in Corinth.[3] But he would have none of the money of the narrow element in

[1] 1 Cor. ix. 6–18. [2] 2 Cor. xi. 5–12. [3] Acts xviii. 3f.

Corinth.[1] On the other hand, some of the Church in Corinth accused Paul of sending Titus to raise the collection for himself.[2] Paul, they said, was the chief "poor saint" for whom the collection was designed. His motives were impugned from every standpoint. He was called a worldly man[3] and an interloper[4] also. But, while all this we know, Paul did not give up the ministry. He was disheartened, too discouraged to work at Troas, but it was due to the very intensity of his interest in the cause of Christ, not to his indifference nor selfishness. If he could not stay at Troas, he could go on elsewhere.

3. *The Gloomy Journey to Macedonia*

It was with a heavy heart that Paul turned away from the open door in Troas to push on into the uncertain future. "But taking leave of them I went forth into Macedonia."[5] There were, then, disciples at Troas. It was probably a journey alone. He could take ship at Troas for Neapolis and then go on to Philippi. At Philippi was Luke in all likelihood. It is possible, even probable, that Titus was the brother of Luke.[6] But Paul's mind doubtless conjured up all the evil contingencies at Corinth.

[1] 2 Cor. xi. 10.
[2] 2 Cor. xii. 16 ff.
[3] 2 Cor. x. 3.
[4] 2 Cor. x. 14 f.
[5] 2 Cor. ii. 13. He made an orderly and courteous departure.
[6] 2 Cor. viii. 16, 18; xii. 18. Titus is not mentioned in Acts. Cf. Souter. "Luke," in Hastings's D. C. G.

The ship went all too slowly for him. "For even when we were come into Macedonia our flesh had no relief, but we were afflicted on every side; without were fightings, within were fears."[1] Much as Paul longed to see Titus, he yet dreaded to hear his report. Suppose the Church has refused to recede from its position? The matters at Corinth had narrowed down to a Pauline and an anti-Pauline contest. His whole position and influence as an apostle were involved. How had they taken the rather sharp[2] letter which he had felt compelled to write? He went on to Philippi with the clouds of doubt about his head and premonition in his heart. This time he speaks of his flesh[3] as having no rest on the way. He had found that unrest of spirit brought unrest to the flesh in sleepless nights, and miserable days. He knew what insomnia[4] was. He has had this restlessness of mind and body all the way.[5] In truth the voyage was one of affliction in everything.[6] He had reached the stage when nothing agreed with him. All the world seemed awry and he could not set it right. He was out of tune with everything. What he means by "fightings without,"[7] we do not

[1] 2 Cor. vii. 5. [2] 2 Cor. vii. 8. [3] 2 Cor. vii. 5.
[4] 2 Cor. vi. 5; cf. 2 Cor. xi. 27.
[5] 2 Cor. vii. 5. Present perfect tense.
[6] Note the anacoluthon due to Paul's passion.
[7] 2 Cor. vii. 5.

know. The words suggest actual conflicts of some sort. He had fights with "wild beasts at Ephesus,"[1] probably referring to his enemies. Perhaps on board the ship Paul encountered some old or new enemies (Jews, Gentiles, or Judaizers), for he had many kinds of foes.[2] The "fears within" were the ever present apprehensions. These were his worst foes, those of the mind. It is, in truth, a mournful picture that the great apostle has drawn of himself at this crisis in his life. We see Paul here in his hour of weakness. It is not a just picture of himself which we get, but it is a true portrayal of his outlook on the world at this juncture. There is thus a bond of sympathy between this greatest of all the ministers of Jesus and the humblest one to-day who may be thrown down by the world spirit. If Paul is able to look on the bright side of the preacher's life, he knows what the dark side is. There is plenty of cloud in his life to set off the light. Indeed, when Paul is driven to boast of his work in comparison with that of the Judaizers at Corinth it is the catalogue of his trials which he counts.[3] He has his "prisons," his "stripes," his "shipwreck," his "perils" of various kinds, his "watchings often," his "hunger and thirst." "If I must needs glory, I will glory of the things that concern my weakness." But just now

[1] 1 Cor. xv. 32. [2] 2 Cor. xi. 26. [3] 2 Cor. xi. 23–33.

Paul cannot glory even in his weakness. He cannot glory in anything. He is a broken man, broken in spirit and in body. Who can help Paul now?[1] This is not the time for Paul to take stock of his ministry.

4. *The Rebound of Heart at Philippi*

Without a word of explanation Paul leaps out of the Slough of Despond and springs like a bird to the heights of joy.[2] He soars aloft like an eagle with proud scorn of the valley beneath him. "But thanks be unto God who always leadeth us in triumph in Christ."[3] A high-strung nature like that of Paul is capable of such extremes of emotion. Laughter and tears lie close to each other. Joy lives next door to sorrow, ay, in the same house and heart. Many a preacher can bear glad testimony to the psychological correctness of Paul's description of his sudden transition from night to day. We are accustomed to sudden, even violent, digressions[4] in Paul's writings, and the matter, in the light of his relations with

[1] 2 Cor. xi. 29.

[2] Bachmann, *Der Zweite Brief des Paulus an die Korinther.* S. 124, says: "Aus der Tiefe in die Höhe."

[3] 2 Cor. ii. 14.

[4] "Instead of giving details of the information which Titus brought to him in Macedonia (vii. 6), he bursts out into a characteristic doxology, which leads him into a long digression, the main topic of the epistle not coming into view again until vi. 11." Bernard, "Expositor's Greek Testament," *in loco.*

Corinth, would be sufficiently clear from the knowledge that Titus met Paul in Philippi with better news from Corinth than he had anticipated. At once the clouds had lifted and the sky was clear again. But, at this point in the Epistle, Paul is completely carried away with joy at the coming of Titus, too entirely swept off into rhapsody to make any explanation of his emotions. He does make the explanation later in the Epistle [1] after he has come back to earth. It is just this rhapsody with which this book is concerned, but, before proceeding with that, it will be well to notice Paul's explanation of his state of exaltation. "Nevertheless He that comforteth the lowly, even God, comforted us by the coming of Titus." [2] The word "comfort" [3] is a common one, particularly in this Epistle. It combines the notions of exhortation and consolation. Paul was glad to see Titus, for he dearly loved this son in the gospel, his "true child after a common faith," [4] but he was even more rejoiced at the news which he bore: "And not by his coming only, but also by the comfort wherewith he was comforted in you, while he told us your longing, your mourning, your zeal for me; so that I rejoiced yet more." [5] The "longing" [6] was to see Paul

[1] 2 Cor. vii. 5–16. [2] 2 Cor. vii. 6. [3] Call to one's side.
[4] Titus i. 4. [5] 2 Cor. vii. 7.
[6] Eager longing in the Greek. Cf. Phil. i. 8.

and it was music to his ears to hear a message like that from Corinth after all that had passed. Possibly Paul made Titus tell it over again [1] with all the details, the names, what they said, etc. It was a charming story to recount, as many a true pastor knows, especially after troubles have come. The "mourning" [2] was due to the rebuke sent by Titus. As a result of the rebuke and the sorrow had come "zeal" [3] for Paul and the cause that Paul stood for. Paul had known that the sharp tone of the Epistle would wound many of them. It had cost him bitter tears [4] to write it. The pang of those sharp words that had to be spoken was part of Paul's misery. Indeed, he had regretted [5] that he had written it, after it was gone and it was too late. But Paul's sorrow is turned into joy. "I now rejoice, not that ye were made sorry, but that ye were made sorry unto repentance." [6] The sorrow was of a godly [7] sort since it bore fruit in a change of mind and life. Hence Paul had really done them no harm. So Paul was comforted and it did his soul good to see "the joy of Titus,[8] because his spirit hath been refreshed

[1] Present participle, possibly repetition.
[2] Cf. Matt. ii. 18.
[3] The same word has a bad sense in 2 Cor. xii. 20.
[4] 2 Cor. ii. 4. He wrote with "tightness of heart."
[5] 2 Cor. vii. 8.
[6] 2 Cor. vii. 9. Note the difference between "sorrow" and "repentance."
[7] According to God's standard.
[8] 2 Cor. vii. 13.

by you all." The word for "refreshed"[1] is the one used by Jesus in His gracious invitation to the weary and the heavy-laden: "I will give you rest."[2] Paul joys in the joy of Titus, the happiness of an old preacher in a young preacher who has accomplished a most difficult and delicate task. Paul had not indeed wholly given the cause up when he sent Titus and had gloried in some of them to him. He is glad now that his words are more than justified.[3] So then Titus is in a tender mood towards the Corinthians and Paul's own "heart is enlarged" towards them. Indeed, "our mouth is open unto you, O Corinthians."[4] "I rejoice that in everything I am of good courage concerning you."[5] Heart and hope have come back to Paul about Corinth and so about all things. The word for "courage" is the same one used by Luke of Paul when the brethren from Rome, having heard of Paul's arrival, came to meet the party "as far as The Market of Appius and The Three Taverns; whom when Paul saw, he thanked God, and took courage."[6] Few things are sweeter in life than human fellowship. The preacher's life is peculiarly rich in the love of the brethren. This is a large part of his reward. He comes close to the inner life of a man and rare Christian love knits heart

[1] Rest again. [2] Matt. ii. 28. [3] 2 Cor. vii. 14 f.
[4] 2 Cor. vii. 11. [5] 2 Cor. vii. 13. [6] Acts xxviii. 15.

to heart. For the moment Paul forgets that there is a stubborn minority left in the Church at Corinth who have resisted every appeal for conciliation. It was only the majority [1] that had come over to Paul and his view of things. But it was evidently such a strong majority that the Church is saved from schism and the obstinate faction can be handled. Paul will come to pay his respects to this minority led by his malignant enemies, the Judaizers, in the latter part of the Epistle.[2] It is this double aspect of the report of Titus that explains the twofold character of the Epistle. But we are not here concerned with Paul's treatment of this pugnacious element save to express the hope that they came over to his side before he came to Corinth. If they did not, they must have left, for Paul is master of the situation in Acts xx. 2 f. Before leaving the discussion of Paul's situation in Philippi, it is interesting to note that Paul was happy once before when here, even though in prison.[3] The Epistle to the Philippians, which he will write from Rome some years hence, is full of joy and commands to rejoice, though Paul at that time will again be a prisoner. But he is now no longer a prisoner in spirit. He is free as a bird as he shakes off the depression which had chained his spirit to the earth. We owe this matchless discus-

[1] 2 Cor. ii. 5 f. [2] 2 Cor. x–xiii. [3] Acts xvi. 25.

sion[1] of the Christian ministry to the very dejection of heart in Paul. The rebound was as high as the depression had been. The reaction was equal to the action. This digression, as already noted,[2] is really quite distinct from the rest of the Epistle. It is, for all intents and purposes, a separate treatise on the glory of the Christian ministry. The brightness of this glory shines all the more brilliantly against the black cloud of doubt and disaster which immediately precedes this outburst of joy. The troubles in Paul's ministry were real, not merely imaginary. He was a manly man, if ever there was one. His difficulties are real still after he meets Titus, though greatly lessened. He has a new light on the problems at Corinth. That light flashes back over his life and forth into the future. He has a new sense of the relative values of things. Now he is in the right mood to estimate his own ministerial life and that of others. It is a great mistake for any preacher to reach a final conclusion in his moments of despondency. One can see better in the light than in the dark. The light will come if one press on towards it. The young man who is struggling with the sense of duty that calls him to be a preacher of the Gospel will be wise if he gives himself a chance to get this high view of the ministry as set

[1] 2 Cor. ii. 12–vi. 10.

[2] See beginning of this section.

forth by Paul in his moment of ecstasy. The highest is the truest as well as the best. The temptation is easy to settle the question of being a preacher on the dead-level of business, expediency, and convenience. I do not believe that many young men will be led into the ministry by mathematical computations on the cost of living and the salary nor on the relations of modern thought to the Bible. No real "Sky-pilot" is ever found with that calculating spirit. It is the spiritual view of the eternal values as seen by Paul in this prophetic passage that will win and hold the noblest type of man to the service of Christ. Nothing else will really get its grip on him. Get into close grip with Christ, if He is tugging at your heart to put you into the ministry. If Christ puts you in, you will stay in and you will not be sorry, but count it your chief glory to have been counted worthy of that high dignity.[1] It is probably true that the ministry to-day does not stand as high relatively in the eyes of men as it once did. This may be due partly to the presence of some unworthy men in the ministry. There was a Judas among the apostles. There have always been unworthy men in every calling. But it hurts more in the ministry than anywhere else. But, after all, Paul does not here speak of the appeal that the ministry makes to

[1] 2 Tim. i. 12.

the world. He gives God's view of the ministry. If one has that, nothing else really matters. "Let a man so account of us, as of ministers of Christ, and stewards of the mysteries of God. . . . But with me it is a very small thing that I should be judged of you, or of man's judgment . . . He that judgeth me is the Lord."[1] So Paul is going to sing a pæan of praise for the ministry. Hear what he has to say of the appeal that this noblest of earth's vocations makes to him. What is it in the ministry that gripped and held a man so gifted as Paul?

5. *The New Interpretation of Paul's Ministry*

He has a new standpoint. The sun often shines on the mountain when it is dark in the valley. Paul is here sheer above the clouds. He can see far and near, up and down, in the clear empyrean. The obstacles that seemed so large in his path have now disappeared wholly from view or have assumed their true proportion in this fresh world-view. Let us stand upon the mountain with Paul and catch his view of the worth and dignity of service to Christ. Paul begins with the interpretation of his own ministry in view of the new light and outlook, but he soon widens his horizon to include the ministry as a calling and he treats it in its fundamental and

[1] 1 Cor. iv. 1–4.

eternal relations in a way to cheer every preacher's heart.

(*a*) *Triumph After All.* But God's triumph, not Paul's. Paul is Christ's captive in God's triumphal march through the ages. God "always leadeth us in triumph in Christ."[1] There is no doubt as to the meaning of this bold image. It does not mean "causeth us to triumph" as the King James' Version has it. No instance of this sense of the word has been found, and in Col. ii. 15 Paul uses it of Jesus "triumphing over them in it," His victory on the cross over the principalities and powers.[2] "He is the captive who is led in the Conqueror's train, and in whom men see the trophy of the Conqueror's power."[3] It is the splendid image of a Roman triumphal procession, and, though Paul had not seen one, he had yet heard of its glories.[4] Distinguished captives were sometimes kept at Rome for years in order to grace the conqueror's procession when it took place. Thus Julius Cæsar held Vercingetorix, the famous chief in Gaul who came near plucking victory out of Cæsar's hands, a prisoner in Rome for six years until his great triumph. Then he had him slain. So Claudius[5]

[1] 2 Cor. ii. 14.
[2] For the examples in Greek literature see Bachmann, 2 Kor., S. 129.
[3] Denney, "Expositor's Bible," 2 Corinthians, p. 87.
[4] Bernard, "Expositor's Greek Testament," *in loco*.
[5] Denney, p. 88.

triumphed over Caractacus. Paul may have had this very occasion in mind. But Paul's case is not quite parallel to that of Vercingetorix or Caractacus. "When God wins a victory over man, and leads His captive in triumph, the captive too has an interest in what happens; it is the beginning of all triumphs, in any true sense, for him."[1] Even in Paul's tribulations and disappointments God has been victorious. It is easier to see the hand of God after we have passed through a crisis. Prof. David Smith, D. D., in a New Year's article in *The British Weekly*[2] pictures a captain looking one morning at the terrible crags on each side of the narrow pass through which the ship had passed in the storm at night into the harbour. "Did we—did we pass through in the darkness?" he falteringly asked. God was using Paul for His glory in it all. Indeed, he dares say "always" now. What seemed to be defeat he now knows is victory. The good news brought by Titus has thrown an electric flashlight across the stormy billows and has revealed God—

> "Standeth God within the shadows
> Keeping watch above His own."

The sense of the nearness of God in his own life and ministry is the overmastering conviction of Paul. He

[1] Denney, p. 88.

[2] Dec. 29, 1910.

probably means to include Timothy[1] and Titus[2] in the "us." Indeed, he seems to have a vision of the whole long line of willing captives of God through the ages, past and present, who have been instruments in pushing on the work of the kingdom.[3] If Paul is able to find joy in the midst of his misfortunes, he has pointed the way for every preacher of Christ. The secret lies in looking at one's life from God's standpoint. But this is only possible "in Christ." "Christ is the element in which that constant triumph of God takes place."[4] F. W. Robertson is right: "The defeat of the true-hearted is victory."[5] It is the joy of full surrender to Christ that Paul here feels. He has cut loose from the entanglement of things of sense and has swung back to the old joy in Jesus.

(*b*) *The Incense Bearer.* Plutarch[6] says that at the Roman triumph the temples were "full of fumigations."[7] "Incense was burned before the victor's chariot."[8] The transition is a very natural one, therefore, for Paul. He now thinks of himself, and all ministers of Christ, as incense bearers in God's march of victory. He "maketh manifest through us

[1] 2 Cor. i. 1.
[2] 2 Cor. ii. 13; vii. 5 ff.
[3] Meyer, 2 Corinthians, *in loco.*
[4] *Ibid.*
[5] "Life and Letters and Addresses," p. 618.
[6] Aemil. Paul., C. 32.
[7] "Incense smoked on every altar as the victor passed through the streets of Rome." Denney, *in loco.*
[8] Gould, American Comm., *in loco.*

the savour of His knowledge in every place." The "savour" and the "knowledge" are in opposition.[1] The knowledge of God in Christ is thus diffused like sweet perfume along the triumphal way of God. But the wonder of it is that the fragrance is spread "through us." This is due to no merit in the minister, but to the fact that he is near to God because he is in the procession so rich in the grace of God. But there is a sense of humble gratitude on Paul's part as he contemplates the great honour thus placed upon him and other preachers of the Gospel, that of spreading the knowledge of God along the way. Preaching[2] is the thing most immediately in Paul's mind, but he quickly turns the image round. "For we are a sweet savour of Christ unto God."[3] He doubtless means that the incense bearer is so filled with the perfume that he himself is perfume. The preacher is so filled with Christ[4] that he exhales Christ. The figure is common in the Old Testament.[5] The life of the true minister of Christ is thus redolent with that "odour of sanctity" which refreshes the heart. But "the lowliest life which God is really leading in triumph will speak infallibly and persuasively for Him."[6] This is true of every follower

[1] Genitive of apposition.

[2] "In every place," also; at Corinth as at Ephesus.

[3] 2 Cor. ii. 15.

[4] Meyer, *in loco.*

[5] Cf. Lev. i. 9, 13, etc.

[6] Denney, *in loco.*

of Jesus who bears witness to Christ in his life. It is usually true that men are responsive to the pervasive influence of holy living and clear testimony to Jesus. But it is not always true. The scribes and Pharisees found fault with John and with Jesus. Paul found it impossible to please all men, though he laboured to be "all things to all men, that I may by all means save some."[1] It had recently seemed to Paul that he was misunderstood on every hand. He now knows better. He still has plenty of enemies who are only too glad to turn any slip on his part to his hurt. Paul is careful "to cut off occasion from them that desire an occasion."[2] As I write these words, I am concerned about the complete misapprehension of the conduct of one of the noblest of ministers. One brother writes me that it is enough to make one lose faith in the ministry! This very brother who so writes is largely responsible for the conduct of the minister whom he so severely criticizes. But Paul has one supreme consolation that is open to us all. It is found in the words "unto God." It is a joy to God, whatever men think, when a life manifests Christ. That life is redolent to God of Christ.

(*c*) *The Peril of Preaching.* The joy is mixed with sadness, for all are not saved. God is, however, glorified "in them that are saved, and in them that

[1] 1 Cor. ix. 22.

[2] 2 Cor. xi. 12.

perish; to the one a savour from death unto death; to the other a savour of life unto life."[1] Paul knew by sad experience the hardening effect of preaching that was resisted. Among those who were perishing[2] right before his eyes Paul and his ministry seemed like a "savour from death unto death."[3] The idiom is a bit obscure, but is like "from faith to faith."[4] This odour arises from death and causes death.[5] The rabbis "called the Law an *aroma vitæ* to the good, but an *aroma mortis* to the evil."[6] The figure was thus one familiar to Paul in his old life. It is a sad thought to every faithful minister to know that men who hear his message will be hardened in sin by it because they reject it. But that is the inevitable penalty of human freedom. On the other hand, there is a bright side to the picture, for "in them that are saved" Paul is "a savour from life unto life."[7] There is progress out of life into more life. There is no joy comparable to that of witnessing the conversion of souls under one's own ministry. This was the joy of Jesus[8] and it is possible for us to have it. A ministry in which souls are not saved misses the chief joy of service. It is small wonder that, in view of the solemn responsibility of such a ministry,

[1] 2 Cor. ii. 15 f.
[2] Present participle in the Greek.
[3] Here not "sweet odour."
[4] Rom. i. 17; cf. 2 Cor. iii. 18.
[5] Meyer, *in loco.*
[6] Bernard, *in loco.*
[7] Present participle in the Greek.
[8] John iv. 32.

Paul asks: "And who is sufficient for these things?" The Greek order is even more emphatic: "And for these things who is sufficient?" He has sketched in the bold contrast of life and death "these things." The word "sufficient" means "fit" or "qualified." Many a preacher has felt his utter inadequacy to meet such a situation. He has arrived, but he is not ready for his task. The stoutest heart may well sink before the work of the modern minister. It is difficult enough in the nature of the case, but people make all sorts of unreasonable demands of preachers. One can become a sort of packhorse for the community's burdens and difficulties. The question of Paul seems rhetorical and to call for the answer that no one is sufficient for such a life as this fraught with such awful consequences for weal or woe.[1] But Paul often surprises us by the bold turn of his thought.

(*d*) *Paul's Courage in Preaching*. He dares to say that he is "sufficient for these things"! "For we are not as the many, corrupting the Word of God." He probably has in mind the Judaizers who did corrupt the Word of God. By "the many" Paul does not mean that the majority were like the Judaizers. They were many, as a matter of fact, but the majority held with Paul. Paul is not now under the juniper tree. He does not feel that he alone is

[1] Bernard, *in loco*.

loyal to Christ. He is not bringing an indictment against the ministers of Christ as a class. He is exposing the hypocrites who had crept into the ministry, as they still do, alas! The word for "corrupting" is used either for a retailer or a huckster. It comes to mean "adulterate," for the temptation was often yielded to then as now, to put the best apples on top of the barrel, the best strawberries on top of the basket. The Judaizers made a plausible plea and show. Paul, in contrast, grounds his confidence on two reasons. One is his sincerity. His berries are as good at the bottom as at the top. He is not afraid to face men with the gospel message, for it is sound to the core. He is not afraid that something will be found out to make him ashamed. He preaches a whole gospel with no mental reservations and a pure gospel with no flaws. In one of the visions of Ezekiel (viii. 7–13) there is a vivid picture of the betrayal of God by His ministers. Ezekiel saw a hole in the wall and he went through and found a door. He went in and he found "every form of creeping things, and abominable beasts, and all the idols of the house of Israel portrayed upon the wall round about. And there stood before them seventy men of the elders of the house of Israel." Then Jehovah said unto Ezekiel: "Son of man, hast thou seen what the elders of the house of Israel do in the dark, every man in his chambers of imagery? for they say, Jehovah seeth us not; Jehovah hath forsaken the land." Alas, and alas! The other reason of Paul is that he bears God's commission. He did not appoint himself to this task. In fact, he was seized in spite of himself and turned round when he was doing his utmost against Christ. "As of God, in the sight of God, speak we in Christ." He multiplies words and turns the idea over like a diamond. He looks at it from various sides. God is the source of his authority. He speaks with the eye of God on him. He speaks in the sphere of Christ. He never goes beyond Christ. He has not yet exhausted the riches of Christ. It is just "the unsearchable riches of Christ" that forever challenge him. He can never tell that news often enough. He, less than the least of the saints, is not worthy to bear that story to the Gentiles. He is not sufficient of himself to face any one with this message, nor is any one sufficient in himself. "But our sufficiency is from God; who also made us sufficient as ministers of a new covenant; not of the letter, but of the spirit." God brought Paul and the rest into the ministry and equipped them for the service. "Such confidence have we through Christ to Godward." It is not self-complacency, but trust in God that fills Paul with holy courage to face a hostile and unbelieving world with the story of redemption in Christ Jesus. The Corinthians ought not to misunderstand him. He is not praising himself. He needs no letter of introduction to them as Apollos had, for instance, when he went to see them, or as the Judaizers may have claimed to have. His work in Corinth is an open letter to be read of all men. A letter of introduction is after all a very cold and lifeless thing. It implies that one is a stranger. But the Corinthians, with all their shortcomings, are written in Paul's very heart. The pastor who reads this bears witness to the truth of Paul's words as he calls up the faces of friends tried and true in this church or in that who have been bound to him with hooks of steel "in Christ."

II

THE GLORY THAT FADED—THE MODERN PROBLEM

(*2 Cor. iii. 6–16*)

"Moses, who put a veil upon his face."
—*2 Cor. iii. 13.*

II

THE GLORY THAT FADED—THE MODERN PROBLEM

PAUL is reminded of the ministry of Moses as representative of the Old Covenant, probably because of the activity of the Judaizers in Corinth who claimed to be the exponents of Mosaism. It is thus an indirect polemic against the Jewish propagandists.[1] But it is more than mere allegorizing,[2] a method that Paul knew how to use on occasion.[3] But, in the present instance, Paul keeps close to the historical situation in Exodus xxiv.–xxxiv. and draws a wonderful parallel in the Judaism of his day. The whole system of Judaism is set in the boldest contrast to the ideal ministry of the New Covenant. This passage is worthy of the closest study by the preacher of to-day whose vision of the spiritual ministry is beclouded by sacerdotalism and ceremonialism. It is pathetic to think that, in spite of Paul's bold and unanswerable exposure of the weakness of a mere sacerdotal ecclesiasticism, to-day in the Greek and Roman Churches are to be found just

[1] Meyer, *in loco*, foot-note. [2] Bernard, *in loco*.
[3] I Cor. x. 2; Gal. iv. 25.

the Jewish conception of the ministry which Paul is condemning. It is undoubtedly true also that the wide-spread influence of these two great Churches has in large measure shaped popular opinion of the minister as priest and cleric rather than as prophet, herald, servant, teacher, pastor. The downfall, the inevitable downfall, of this Jewish conception has brought untold harm to the ministry *per se*. It is not easy for people to distinguish. The pinnacle upon which Paul places the preacher is not one of officialism in any sense. He is the man of high spiritual prerogative and privilege, not the man of ecclesiastical station. He is the man who looks in the face of God and comes to talk with the people as prophet, not as priest nor ecclesiastic. The problem before Paul is intensely modern in many of its phases. The ministry to-day has lost its glory for many people. There was once a halo about the calling of the minister which to some is now lost. It was once the dearest hope in every Scottish home, as in many others all over the world, that the boy would become a minister of Jesus Christ. Ian Maclaren has told with tender pathos how the cold blast of modern criticism has smitten this fair flower of faith in Bonnie Scotland.[1] Numerous modern novels seek to justify the modern denial of Jesus in its appeal to

[1] "Beside the Bonnie Briar Bush."

the youth of to-day.[1] Paul graphically seizes upon the picture of Moses on Mount Sinai and uses it with powerful effect.

1. *A Real Glory*

Paul does not at all mean to deny the fact of the glory that belonged to Moses. The coming of the law was with glory.[2] Indeed, the ministry of the Old Covenant was glory.[3] "The glory of Jehovah abode upon Mount Sinai, and the cloud covered it six days; and the seventh day He called unto Moses out of the midst of the cloud."[4] These forty days and forty nights of communion with God left a mark of external radiance on the face of Moses. The divine glory was on the face of Moses. It is told with wonderful simplicity and power. "And it came to pass, when Moses came down from Mount Sinai with the two tables of the testimony in Moses' hand, when he came down from the mount, that Moses knew not that the skin of his face shone by reason of his speaking with Him."[5] The charm lies in the unconsciousness of Moses. The "God of glory"[6] had appeared unto Abraham as He did to Stephen whose face shone like that of an angel[7] as he began to speak. It has sometimes happened that

[1] Cf. "Robert Elsmere."
[2] 2 Cor. iii. 7.
[3] 2 Cor. iii. 9.
[4] Ex. xxiv. 16.
[5] Ex. xxxiv. 29.
[6] Acts vii. 2; Gen. xii. 1.
[7] Acts vi. 15; vii. 1 f.

the modern minister comes to the pulpit from the throne of grace with the glory of God on his face. He is himself all unconscious of his heavenly radiance as he breaks the bread of life to the people. But they know it and thank God for the testimony in their hearts. "And when Aaron and all the children of Israel saw Moses, behold, the skin of his face shone; and they were afraid to come nigh him."[1] They felt a solemn awe in his presence. They felt in truth the other Presence, the Presence of God in manifest power and glory. The rabbis had a fiction that this glory was from the light of creation,[2] but that is mere trifling. It was the ineffable glory in which Jehovah dwells that filled the countenance of Moses. It is the highest crown of the minister that he is called so often into the closest fellowship with the Eternal God. There is, of course, no special ministerial approach to the Throne of God, but his very work of itself draws him to communion with God. A preacher may not live up to his rich privilege, but it is there for him. There is no way to put on this radiant glory, no way but the "Practice of the Presence of God." Moses had actually been with God. He had to call Aaron and the rest to his side and they gradually drew nigh and listened

[1] Ex. xxxiv. 30.
[2] Meyer, *in loco;* Eisenmenger, *Entdeckt. Judenth.*, I., S. 369 f.

to his message from God.[1] It is a moment of unspeakable responsibility when a man's soul is ablaze with the Word of God and his audience are " in tune with the infinite." Then the deepest mark is made upon the soul. There are mountain peaks in the experience of most men when the tongue is touched by the coal from the altar of God.[2] Then one is able to " cry " with power.[3] It is at such supreme moments that souls are born into the kingdom, that men are called into the ministry. John A. Broadus had expected to be a physician and was studying towards that end, but he heard A. M. Poindexter preach one day on the " Parable of the Talents," and he could never get away from that sermon. It sent him into the ministry.[4] It may be questioned if Dr. Poindexter ever performed a more useful service in his life than the preaching of this sermon. There is still glory and power in the ministry under God. One way to enlist more men in the work of the ministry is to pray for more labourers as Jesus commanded.[5] Another way is to live close to God and preach with the power and demonstration of the Spirit. Paul gathered many young ministers about him, like Timothy and Titus, who were a joy to his heart. But the man wins more men to

[1] Ex. xxxiv. 31 f. [2] Isa. vi. 6 ff. [3] Isa. xl. 6.
[4] Robertson, " Life and Letters of John A. Broadus," p. 52 f.
[5] Matt. ix. 38 ; Luke x. 2.

the ministry who is unconscious of any special halo on his own head. He sees only the face of Jesus his Lord. Syria was once "the Cradle of the Prophets."[1] That is no longer the case, but it is an honour to a church or a land to be a "hot-bed for preachers."

2. *A Hidden Glory*

"And when Moses had done speaking with them he put a veil on his face."[2] Paul interprets it thus: "so that the children of Israel could not look steadfastly upon the face of Moses for the glory of his face."[3] They felt as if they were looking right at the sun and they could not stand the brilliant light. Indeed, the sun will put out the eyes of those who dare to gaze directly at his light for long. We resort to smoked glasses or take advantage of an eclipse to look steadfastly in the face of the sun. So Moses took the veil off only when he went in to speak with the Lord and put it on when he came out to speak with the people.[4] There was a great gulf between the people and Moses. "Judaism had the one lawgiver who beheld God while the people tarried below. Christianity leads us all to the mount of vision, and lets the lowliest pass through the fences, and go up where the blazing glory is seen. Moses veiled the

[1] *The Intercollegian*, Jan., 1911, p. 86.
[2] Ex. xxxiv. 33.
[3] 2 Cor. iii. 7.
[4] Ex. xxxiv. 34 f.

face that shone with the irradiation of Deity. We with unveiled face are to shine among men."[1] Maclaren[2] is right also in saying that Paul's habit of "going off at a word," as illustrated in this passage about Moses and the veil, is not a mark of confusion, but "of the fervid richness of the apostle's mind, which acquires force by motion, and, like a chariot-wheel, catches fire as it revolves." So, he continues, in this scene on the mount, "we have a picture of the Old Dispensation—a partial revelation, gleaming through a veil, flashing through symbols, expressed here in a rite, there in a type, there again in an obscure prophecy, but never or scarcely ever fronting the world with an unveiled face and the light of God shining clear from it. Christianity is, and Christian teachers ought to be, the opposite of all this. It has, and they are to have, no esoteric doctrines, no hints where plain speech is possible, no reserve, no use of symbols and ceremonies to overlay truth, but an intelligible revelation in words and deeds, to men's understandings. It and they are plentifully to declare the thing as it is." Paul means to cast no reproach upon Moses or the Old Covenant by this contrast. The people simply could not stand the fullness of light which Moses had. Even if it was

[1] Maclaren, "Expositions of Holy Scripture," 2 Corinthians, *in loco.*
[2] *Ibid.*

merely the skin of his face that shone with external glory, it was too bright for their eyes since they did not enjoy the inner light of Christianity. The charge is sometimes made to-day against the ministry that it is the profession of obscurantists. Either modern ministers are dishonest in not being true to what they know and pander to the ignorance of the people or they have closed their minds to all light and progress. Both of these charges are freely made in some quarters and occasionally some colour is given to it by a minister whose defection is made a newspaper sensation. Notoriety always comes to the preacher who betrays his Lord or his gospel. As a result some young men are made to believe that the ministry is an unworthy calling for a free man who does not wish to wear shackles. Hear Lord Morley, for instance, in his famous essay on *Compromise:* "These cases only show the essential and profound immorality of the priestly profession, which makes a man's living depend on his abstaining from using his mind, or concealing the conclusions to which the use of his mind has brought him. The time will come when society will look back on the doctrine that they that serve the altar shall live by the altar as a doctrine of barbarism and degradation." Lord Morley is an outspoken free-thinker and agnostic, and his indictment of the ministry can thus be discounted. But the matter is taken very seriously by Rev. Canon Danks,[1] of the Church of England, who calls them "words of very serious import to men who have entered or who wish to enter the ministry." He says: "They express the thought which, more than any other cause, deters able candidates for ordination. Nor has their force been lessened by the lapse of time, for the gap between the critics and the popular theology is wider now than thirty-five years ago. . . . There is a greater gulf between the theological student and the untaught believer or unbeliever than ever before." It is evident that such a situation exists in many quarters and the wide-spread decrease in the number of students for the ministry, once so serious and now happily disappearing, may be partly due to this cause. Dr. Danks has probably somewhat exaggerated its influence, but it is a real problem. He replies in behalf of the Church of England: "Were Hooker and Butler emissaries of intellectual darkness, slaves themselves and enslaving others? Were Thirlwall, Lightfoot, Westcott, Creighton, Robertson of Brighton, Maurice, Kingsley, Stanley, Jowett —were all these obscurantists, stunting the mental growth of their time? On the contrary, they were

[1] Article, "The Clergy, Conscience, and Free Inquiry," *The Hibbert Journal*, Jan., 1911.

among the most alert, profound, and free intelligences of their time, teaching and emancipating their own and succeeding generations. Nor is there, so far as I know, any reason to suppose that they were in the least conscious of thinking in fetters, or acting a part." This is a pertinent reply. Indeed, the fault found to-day with many men in the ministry is not that they are "hidebound reactionaries," but that they are entirely too advanced and radical. But their very presence and work constitute an answer to Lord Morley's charge. Moses was at first unconscious of the glory on his face, but the conduct of the people made him aware of the radiance. It was not acting a part to hide his face with the veil. He delivered his message with covered face. It is no deception for the minister to-day to keep his inmost self to himself. He does not claim omniscience. If new light is coming, more may come. Modesty is becoming to the herald of the Cross. He is not called upon to parade his doubts nor all the hidden ecstasies of his life with God. He must be willing to wait and learn like other men. One should preach his beliefs, not his doubts. But, when a real breach has come between him and Christ, he is not called upon to act the hypocrite and to go on mumbling phrases and words that have no meaning to him. The door is still open for him to go out of the ministry of Christ when there is no freedom within it. He must be his own judge when to keep still on less important matters and when to speak his mind on vital issues. But there is never reason for whimperings on the limitations of the ministry; never, unless one is in the grip of a priestly hierarchy. Then, much of what Lord Morley says is true. There is to-day a movement in the Roman Catholic Church called "Modernism." It has aroused the wrath of Pope Pius X to such an extent that he has turned the whole power of the Vatican to its destruction.[1] The outcome no one can tell, but "what we can foresee is this, that it will be one of the most momentous crises recorded in history."[2] It is chiefly because Romanism has sought to put clamps upon the human spirit, as the later Judaism of Paul's day did, that this crisis has come. Protestantism stands out against medieval Romanism as Paul's interpretation of a free Christianity rises above the fettered Judaism of his time which he once proclaimed and sought to force upon the Christians themselves. A group of Roman Catholic priests in Italy have addressed a

[1] He has issued a Syllabus, two Encyclicals (1907, 1909), and in September, 1910, used the *Motu proprio* to compel every professor, every new confessor, priest, and canon to take the oath of orthodoxy.

[2] Prof. Giovanni Luzzi, D. D., Florence, in the January, 1911, *Hibbert Journal*, article, "The Roman Catholic Church in Italy at the Present Hour."

letter to Pius X entitled "*What we want,*"[1] in which they say: "Our society has now for many years held entirely aloof from the Church, which it considers as an ancient and inexorable foe. . . . The Church is considered an obstacle to the happiness of nations; the priest is insulted in public as a common, ignorant parasite; the Gospel and Christianity are regarded as expressions of a decayed civilization, because they are entirely insufficient to answer to the ideals of freedom, justice, and science which are shaking the masses." This portrayal does not come from Lord Morley, but is the despairing cry of Roman Catholic priests about Romanism. The trouble is just here that men do not always distinguish between priest and preacher. Paul is not in his noble panegyric on the ministry calling men to the decayed Judaism nor to the corrupt and corrupting Romanism of the future, but to the glorious Gospel of the Son of God which is not bound.[2] Men could bind Paul, but not the gospel of the kingdom. He was bound in the spirit with allegiance to Christ, but had no fear of man.[3] Jesus had said that the truth would make men free. It was God's purpose to give the world a message which would be

[1] *Quel che vogliano.* Quoted by Professor Luzzi in the *Hibbert Journal* article.
[2] 2 Tim. ii. 9. [3] Acts xx. 23.

delivered boldly and openly without any veil upon the face. "Having therefore such a hope, we use great boldness of speech, and are not as Moses, who put a veil upon his face."[1] The word "boldness" means "telling it all."[2] Paul glories in his freedom as a minister of Christ. God has come in Christ and the Light has been tempered to the eye of man.

3. *A Temporary Glory*

Paul expressly calls attention to the transient aspect of the glory on the face of Moses as a symbol of the passing glory of the Mosaic ministry and so of Judaism—"Moses, who put a veil upon his face, that the children of Israel should not look steadfastly on the end of that which was passing away."[3] So in verse seven he says: "Which glory was passing away." Meyer[4] takes Paul's language to mean that Moses practiced "dissembling" with the people since he did not wish the people to see the glory on his face die away, else they would lose respect for him and his work. However, he does not think that Paul regarded this act as immoral on the part of Moses. Paul is not in verse thirteen denying what he said in verse seven about the light being too bril-

[1] 2 Cor. iii. 12.
[2] Cf. John vii. 13 where it is translated "openly."
[3] 2 Cor. iii. 13.
[4] *In loco.*

liant for the people to look upon.[1] The language in verse thirteen undoubtedly presents a purpose to prevent the people of Israel from seeing the departure of the glory on the countenance of Moses.[2] Some have even supposed that Christ is meant by "the end of that which was passing away."[3] But that is quite beside the mark. There is no direct statement in Exodus concerning this second point made by Paul, though the transient nature of the glory on the face of Moses is plain in the context. It is clear in the consciousness of Moses since he kept[4] putting the veil on and off. But one is going far beyond Paul's remarks on the story in Exodus to accuse Moses of dissembling. He probably first put the veil on because the brightness he found "was so resplendent as to dazzle the beholders."[5] Then he realized that, when he did speak to the people without the veil, the people would note that the glory was no longer on his countenance. How long he kept up that plan is not made plain, but the day came, probably soon, when he had to speak without the

[1] Bernard, *in loco*, notes that in Ex. xxxiv. 33 "till" in the Authorized Version has been changed to "when" in the Revised Version. But, even so, that does not affect the two points made by Paul.

[2] "That" is design, not result.

[3] Cf. Rom. x. 4.

[4] 2 Cor. iii. 13.

[5] Denny, 2 Corinthians, *in loco*. For a discussion of the interpretation of the Targums, the Septuagint, and Philo, see Bachmann, *Der Zweite Brief des Paulus an die Korinther*, S. 156

veil. What Moses avoided was the people seeing the glory slowly vanish away each time. There is a real parallel here in the experience of every minister when he has spoken with power concerning the things of God. In the pulpit he has seemed like one inspired. When he steps down among the people, there is need of caution lest a violent nervous reaction may dissipate at once the real spiritual impression produced. A story is told about a famous preacher to the effect that, when he was in the pulpit, the church wished he would never leave it; but, when he was out of it, they wished that he would never enter it. The only way to have permanent glory is to continue beholding the glory of the Lord. If we cease looking at Him, we cease to reflect His glory. Moses may not have thought at all (almost certainly did not) of his conduct being a type of the temporary nature of his ministry, nor was he thinking of the difference between what he was and what he had to teach.[1] A preacher is often tempted to hide his own person and weaknesses out of sight in order to concentrate attention on what he is saying. To a certain extent this is justifiable, but people will not allow a clear divorce between preaching and practice on the part of the minister. "Moses had a momentary gleam, a transient brightness; we have a

[1] Cf. Meyer, *in loco.*

perpetual light. Moses' face shone, but the lustre was but skin deep. But the light that we have is inward, and works transformation into its own likeness."[1] There is a finality in the revelation of the Gospel which is not true of Judaism. "The true greatness of God is revealed, and with it His true glory, once for all, in the Gospel."[2] Paul exults in this surpassing difference: "For if that which passeth away was with glory, much more that which remaineth is in glory."[3] Paul boldly champions the permanence of the glory and service in Christ. The New Testament ministry will continue because there is no higher word for the redemption of man than the Gospel of Christ. Jesus is the fullness of God's message to man. We shall continue to get new light on that message, but shall never get beyond it.[4] The demand for ministers of the Gospel to-day is just the same as it was in the first century. Nor has preaching lost its power over the hearts of men. That is a cry that comes in each generation. Human life takes on new phases. The printing press brings the newspaper, the magazine, and the novel. The telephone, the automobile, the electric car revolutionize the habits of men. But no printed page can per-

[1] Maclaren, "Expositions of Holy Scripture," *in loco.*
[2] Denney, *in loco.* [3] 2 Cor. iii. 11.
[4] Works like G. B. Foster's "Finality of the Christian Religion are mere passing leaves.

manently supply the place of the man who has looked into the face of God and now looks into the face of sinful men and presses home with burning words the sense of sin and the redemption in Jesus Christ. The minister who does this has a great hearing to-day and will always be greeted by glad hearts. This is the eternal call for preachers, the heart-hunger[1] of sinful men for the knowledge of God in Christ, for the unveiling of their real selves, for the touch of heart upon heart, for the mighty moving of the Spirit of God. The greatest spirits of all time have responded to this call of God and will continue to do so. A Protestant scholasticism,[2] a Roman Catholic hierarchy, a Jewish scribism may lose the gift of spiritual insight, of human sympathy, of power to speak for God. But even so God is not bound to this system or to that. He will find men who can hear His voice and see His face.[3]

4. *An Overshadowed Glory*

The glory on the face of Moses passed away, but there was a real glory in the Old Covenant. There was and there still is. It is an argument at first from the less to the greater. "If the ministration of death

[1] Cf. Stalker, "The Preacher and His Models," p. 25 f.
[2] Denney, *in loco.*
[3] Commenting on the coming of the Rev. J. H. Jowett from Birmingham to New York, *The British Weekly*, Jan. 26, 1891, speaks of "The Call for Preachers" and quotes from a saying of

. . . came with glory, how shall not rather the ministration of the spirit be with glory?"[1] The condition admits the glory of the Old Dispensation and by a rhetorical question argues the greater glory of the New Dispensation. "For if the ministration of condemnation hath glory, much rather doth the ministration of righteousness exceed in glory."[2] Paul admits the glory of the Old, but claims the much richer glory of the New. In itself this is no disparagement of the true Judaism. "For if that which passeth away was with glory, much more that which remaineth is in glory."[3] Three times Paul has thus used the argument from the less to the greater. It is a self-evident proposition. But, in truth, there is such an overplus[4] of glory in the New Covenant that the glory of the Old seems to disappear entirely; the greater glory dims the less. "For verily that which hath been made glorious hath not been made glorious in this respect, by reason of the glory that surpasseth."[5] In one point at least the old seems to have no glory at all, because of the superabundant glory of the New Covenant.[6] "The veiled Moses represents

Martin Luther in Dr. Kawerau's tribute to Spurgeon: "In the Church it is not enough that books should be written and read, but it is necessary that there should be speaking and hearing. Therefore Christ wrote nothing, but spoke everything. The apostles wrote little, but spoke a great deal."

[1] 2 Cor. iii. 7 f. [2] 2 Cor. iii. 9. [3] 2 Cor. iii. 11.
[4] 2 Cor. iii. 9. [5] 2 Cor. iii. 10. [6] 2 Cor. iii. 10.

the clouded revelation of old. The vanishing gleam on his face recalls the fading glories of that which was abolished."[1] "The stars are bright till the moon rises; the moon herself reigns in heaven till her splendour pales before the sun; but when the sun shines in his strength, there is no other glory in the sky. All the glories of the Old Covenant have vanished for Paul in the light which shines from the Cross and from the Throne of Christ."[2] Paul had already caught the vision of the conquest of Christianity and of the vanishing of Judaism by comparison. The Jews still linger in the world as a witness of God's Word till the times of the Gentiles be fulfilled.[3] Israel Zangwill[4] even now laments: "What threatens the existence of the race is the decay of Judaism." But with Paul there is no rivalry, so far does Christianity outdistance Judaism. There was no rivalry between John the Baptist and Jesus because John saw clearly that his light was to fade before that of Jesus: "He must increase, but I must decrease."[5] John was the herald of the dawn as the sun arose. The true Judaism finds its fulfillment in Christ.[6] Sometimes a preacher is sorely tested when he sees another minister go far beyond him in use-

[1] Maclaren, "Expositions," *in loco.*
[2] Denney, *in loco.*
[3] Luke xxi. 24; Rom. xi. 25.
[4] *The Jewish Review*, Jan., 1911, p. 391.
[5] John iii. 30.
[6] Rom. x. 4.

fulness and popular favour. His light is dimmed by that of a greater personality. Happy is he if he can rejoice in the greater light, "that he that soweth and he that reapeth may rejoice together."[1] An old minister will do well to watch his spirit and to find joy in the young ministers about him. God will keep our going out into activity and our coming in to the inner shrine.[2] "In that inner room of life there sits Regret with her pale face, and Shame with dust on her forehead, and Memory with tears in her eyes. It is a pitiable thing sometimes, this coming in. More than one man has consumed his life in a flame of activity because he could not abide the coming in. But, 'The Lord shall keep thy coming in'—that means help for every lonely, impotent, inward hour of life."[3] But Paul stands in the full glory of Christianity with naught to conceal. He is not afraid that people will find out something about the Gospel. "St. Paul has painted his own portrait at full length, and in every line of it is the portrait of the minister. There is more in his writings which touches the very quick of our life as ministers than in all other writings in existence."[4] Paul speaks out of his heart for the Christian ministry of all ages

[1] John iv. 36. [2] Cf. Psalm cxxi. 8.
[3] Percy C. Ainsworth, "The Threshold Grace."
[4] Stalker, "The Preacher and His Models," p. 18.

when he exalts Christianity above Judaism and all other religions in the world and places the Christian ministry at the summit of life's callings. Nothing can ever overshadow the true glory of the ministry of Jesus Christ. "If the pulpit has an authentic message to deliver about Him whose thought is the ground of all existence, and whose will of love is the explanation of the pain and mystery of life, the more cultivated and eager the mind of man becomes, then the more indispensable will the voice of the pulpit be felt to be; and a real decay of the power of the pulpit can only be due either to preachers themselves, when, losing touch with the mysteries of revelation, they let themselves down to the level of vendors of passing opinion, or to such a shallowing of the general mind as will render it incapable of taking an earnest interest in the profounder problems of existence."

5. *A Defective Glory*

At its best the Old Covenant had drawbacks of a serious nature in spite of its real glory. It is a ministry of the "letter" as opposed to "spirit." God "made us sufficient as ministers of a new covenant; not of the letter, but of the spirit: for the letter killeth, but the spirit giveth life."[2] It is not entirely

[1] Stalker, "The Preacher and His Models," p. 27.
[2] 2 Cor. iii. 6.

clear what Paul means by these words. Meyer[1] takes it to mean "the *reason* why God hath made them capable of ministering not to the *letter*, but to the *spirit*." Certainly the scribes had made the law a matter of letter and form, not of spiritual life and power. But it is probable that Paul is making a more serious charge than the patent misuse of the law current among the rabbis. In Romans vii. 6 he speaks of serving "in newness of the spirit, and not in oldness of the letter,"[2] as in Romans ii. 29 he describes the "Jew who is one inwardly; and circumcision is that of the heart, in the spirit, not in the letter." He does not mean a contrast between the letter of the law and the spirit of the law. The contrast is drawn between the law as letter and the redeemed spirit in man.[3] The spiritual life is strangled by literalism, but it is not the point aimed at here by Paul.[4] The law is meant by "letter" and works death. We are under the curse of the law when we seek to be saved by the law.[5] Christ has redeemed us from under the curse of the law,[6] having become a curse for us. The Spirit of Christ makes alive our spirits held in the grip of the law which was death. The law, then, kills,[7] while the Spirit quickens.[8]

[1] *In loco.* [2] Cf. Rom. vi. 4. [3] Bernard, *in loco.*
[4] Denney, *in loco.* [5] Gal. iii. 10. [6] Gal. iii. 13.
[7] Cf. Rom. vii. 7-24. [8] Cf. Rom. vii. 25-viii. 11.

"When the apostle has written these two little sentences—when he has supplied 'letter' and 'spirit' with 'kill' and 'make alive,' in the sense which they bear in the Christian revelation—he has gone as far as the mind of man can go in stating an effective contrast." But Paul turns the idea over a few times. He plainly mentions "the ministration of death, written, *and* engraved on stones" in contrast with "the ministration of the spirit."[1] Paul takes up the word "letter" and applies[2] it to the tables of law brought down by Moses on Mount Sinai. The tradition in Philo[3] was that the words were graven on stone, though the narrative in Exodus[4] does not say so. Paul had felt the death-chill of the law in his own life, though the law was good in itself, yet it only brought a keener consciousness of sin.[5] The Old Covenant had merely a "ministration of condemnation" in contrast with "the ministration of righteousness."[6] Paul insists that righteousness is not of the law, but of faith.[7] Satan poses as an angel of light and puts forward his ministers as "ministers of righteousness."[8] But the thunders of Sinai brought only the voice of condemnation. It is all "thou shalt" and "thou shalt not." There is a

[1] 2 Cor. iii. 7 f. [2] 2 Cor. iii. 7. [3] Vita Mos. iii. 2.
[4] Ex. xxxiv. 29. [5] Rom. v. 20 f.; vii. 7–12.
[6] 2 Cor. iii. 9. [7] Gal. iii. 21. [8] 2 Cor. xi. 15.

majesty more transcendent about the New Dispensation,[1] but the dominant note is grace, not law. The ministers of the New Covenant have hope and certainty. They bear a message of cheer, not of mere condemnation. It is still a terrible thing to fall into the hands of the living God after having trodden under foot the Son of God and having done despite unto the Spirit of His grace, more terrible than it was under the Mosaic dispensation.[2] But the minister of Christ is not a mere denouncer of evil, though he has to cry aloud and spare not like the prophets of old. He is the herald of the Gospel, the bearer of pardon to sinners who will respond to the grace of God. This is the greatest difference between the ministers of the Old Covenant and those of the New. "How beautiful are the feet of them that bring glad tidings of good things!"[3] Paul knew this to be true in a sense not understood by Isaiah.[4] It is sad to see a minister of Christ who is still at Sinai, who is still under the Old Covenant, who is still proclaiming the message of death, who has not caught the vision of love and grace and hope in the New Covenant. Paul's appeal is for men who will carry the message of the Cross, not of Sinai. Paul sees in Jesus the emancipation of the human spirit from the

[1] Heb. ii. 1–4; xii. 25–29.
[2] Heb. x. 26–31.
[3] Rom. x. 15.
[4] Isa. lii. 7; cf. Nahum i. 15.

250
SL 63

17

Eph 4:11-16

bondage of the law. The chill of mere formalism had frozen the life out of Judaism as it has destroyed the real power of many expressions of Christianity. There is to-day the same peril in sacerdotalism that Paul feared in Judaism. The emptiness of mere negative rules was abhorrent to his free spirit. He had known by bitter experience the dry-rot of mere religiosity and sanctimoniousness. Professional sanctity was repellent to Paul's nature. He saw in the Christian ministry the exponents of God's love and of personal piety. No greater peril confronts the minister to-day than the one Paul found in the Judaism of his day. The prophet disappeared in the priest. The priest dried up in the scribe. The scribe split hairs over what prophet and priest had meant. Traditional interpretation took the place of vital experience of God. Love of the external killed the inner life and crucified Jesus of Nazareth for His emphasis on the spiritual life and rebuke of the mere ceremonialism of the scribes and Pharisees. Stephen went the way of Jesus when he rebuked the Pharisees for their perversion of real religion and sought to give the spiritual interpretation of the kingdom of God as expounded by Jesus. Paul turned from persecuting Pharisee to spiritual interpreter of Jesus and took the place of Stephen in whose death he had rejoiced. Jesus and Stephen fought official Pharisaism in the current Judaism. Paul took up the battle with Pharisaism within the Christian fold which was seeking to put the fetters of their perverted Judaism upon the Christianity of Jesus. The one hope of rescue for the soul of man was in jeopardy. Paul's soul was stirred to its depths and he met the issue with all the force of his nature. He is in the thick of the fight with these Judaizing Christians, who were attempting to destroy spiritual Christianity, when he draws the contrast here between Judaism and Christianity. The battle between the bondage of legalism and spiritual Christianity has never ceased. Paul set up his standard in 2 Corinthians, Galatians, Romans. Luther took it up hundreds of years afterwards. The peril is always real. The very difficulties of the struggle challenge great spirits to enter the lists. The evident perversions of Christianity and failure of some ministers to be apostles of freedom in Christ should not repel the best spirits of our time. They should the rather hear the call to fight for the soul of man against all who seek to bind him whether king or priest, state or church, traditionalist or innovationist. The minister will need to keep himself close to God if he is to fight against the mighty forces of reaction and radicalism. Paul had to beat off the Judaizers with their narrowness on the one hand and the Gnostics with their false liberality and philosophic looseness on the other. The preacher of Christ to-day needs constant renewal of his spiritual life to avoid this empty professionalism into which Judaism had sunk. "Valuable as an initial call may be, it will not do to trade too long on such a memory. A ministry of growing power must be one of growing experience. The soul must be in touch with God and enjoy golden hours of fresh revelation. The truth must come to the minister as the satisfaction of his own needs and the answer to his perplexities."[1] Religiosity is not religion.

6. *An Ineffective Glory*

The saddest thing about the history of the Old Covenant was its failure to work the spiritual renewal of the people. The story of Israel till the Captivity is that of desertion of God. The people kept going after the idols of the nations around them in spite of prophets like Samuel, Elijah, Elisha, Isaiah, Jeremiah. After the Restoration the Jews stuck to the letter of the law and missed God again. Hear Paul[2] again: "But their minds were hardened; for until this very day at the reading of the Old Covenant the same veil remaineth, it not being revealed to them

[1] Stalker, "The Preacher and His Models," p. 53.
[2] 2 Cor. iii. 14 f.

that it is done away in Christ. But unto this day, whensoever Moses is read, a veil lieth upon the heart." Moses lived to see the blindness of his people: "But Jehovah hath not given you a heart to know, and eyes to see, and ears to hear, unto this day."[1] Indeed, at Sinai Moses knew when he cried: "Oh, this people have sinned a great sin and have made them gods of gold."[2] But even so Moses loved his people so much that he wished to be blotted out of God's book if God could not forgive them.[3] So Paul felt about the Jews: "I could wish that I myself were anathema from Christ for my brethren's sake, my kinsmen according to the flesh."[4] But Paul knew only too well the tragedy[5] of Judaism, how Jesus came unto His own and His own received Him not.[6] He had himself tried to lift the veil that rested on the heart of the Jews, but had found it very hard to do.[7] They had thrust the Gospel from them and compelled Paul to turn to the Gentiles. Paul knew how bitter it was to preach to an unresponsive audience, whose thoughts were hardened[8] like tough gristle or leather. The veil on the face of Moses had its analogue in a veil on the heart of the people. He had to hide the glory on his face from them and they

[1] Deut. xxix. 4.
[2] Ex. xxxii. 31.
[3] Ex. xxxii. 32.
[4] Rom. ix. 3.
[5] Cf. Conder, "The Hebrew Tragedy."
[6] John i. 11.
[7] Cf. Acts xiii. 44 ff.; xvii. 5; xviii. 14, etc.
[8] 2 Cor. iii. 14.

became unable to see the glory after the other veil was gone. The message of Moses is written in the Old Covenant[1] (Testament), but the people have no eyes to see. The eyes of their heart[2] have not been enlightened that they may know the "riches of the glory of his inheritance in the saints." "But as to Israel he saith, All the day long did I spread out my hands to a disobedient and gainsaying people."[3] Paul found hope in the fact that the Gentiles will hear.[4] Good may come in the end to the Jews who remain.[5] But, meanwhile, the Jews still have the veil on their hearts. Some of them are beginning to see some beauty in Jesus.[6] Others[7] resent this Jewish liberalism as treason to Moses. The breach between the current Judaism and Christianity still exists. But, that is not all. Some ministers find a wider breach between the currents of modern life and the message of Christ. Some, alas, find that the Gospel of Christ no longer charms their own souls, that they have an unresponsive people whose hearts are dead to the spiritual appeal, who are slaves to mammon and greed and who do not love God nor fear man. The light has gone out and the glory has faded from the hills. God pity that preacher and

[1] Cf. Heb. ix. 16 f. [2] Eph. i. 18. [3] Rom. x. 21.
[4] Acts xxviii. 28. [5] Rom. xi.
[6] Cf. Montefiore, "The Religious Teaching of Jesus" (1910).
[7] Cf. *The Jewish Review*, October, 1910.

turn his face towards Jesus. "But whensoever it [the heart] shall turn to the Lord, the veil is taken away."[1] By "Lord" Paul means the Lord Jesus. Christ can lift the veil of spiritual ignorance and indifference from the heart of Jew and Gentile, preacher and people. No one else can do that. What the world to-day needs is the look at Christ, the look of trust with the heart, the turning from Moses and rabbi, from mammon and self, from pride of philosophy and self-righteousness, to the Light that is in the Face of Christ. There and there alone will be found spiritual rejuvenation.

[1] 2 Cor. iii. 16.

III

THE LIGHT IN THE FACE OF JESUS—THE ATTRACTION OF CHRIST

(2 *Cor. iv. 4–6*)

"The light of the knowledge of the glory of God in the face of Jesus Christ."

—*2 Cor. iv. 6.*

III

THE LIGHT IN THE FACE OF JESUS—THE ATTRACTION OF CHRIST

I. *The Face of Jesus Christ*

PAUL did not probably know Jesus in the flesh. He once knew Him "after the flesh,"[1] but that expression almost certainly means that he once looked upon Christ as men of the world still do. He had once hated and persecuted Jesus. It is sometimes objected that Paul discounted the earthly life of Jesus. "He tells us in several places, more especially in the opening chapters of Galatians, that he does not regard the searching out of historic evidence as of any importance."[2] That is surely reading much into Paul. Hear Professor Gardner again: "Within a generation of the Crucifixion we find St. Paul placing the human life of his Master between two periods of celestial exaltation. That was the beginning of Christology." Paul did do that, but so did John's Gospel[3] and Epistles[4] and

[1] 2 Cor. v. 16.
[2] Percy Gardner, in "Jesus or Christ" (*Hibbert Journal Supplement* for 1909), p. 48.
[3] John i. 1–18.
[4] John i. 1–4; cf. "The Face of Jesus," by David Smith.

the Synoptic Gospels and Acts.[1] It is true that Paul cared more about the right interpretation of Jesus and the proper attitude towards Him than he did about the mere historical events of the earthly life of Jesus. But a careful study of Paul's Epistles and his addresses in Acts will show that he knew all the crucial points of that life. Many of these were matters of public knowledge which Paul would have learned during his leadership of the persecution of the Christians in Jerusalem. After his conversion Paul had fifteen days in Jerusalem with Simon Peter right in the midst of the closing scenes of Christ's life.[2] "No one has the right to say that Saul had no knowledge of the historical Jesus. If Luke could learn, so could Paul. Sanday[3] rightly argues that the allusions in Paul's Epistles (cf. 1 Cor. xi. 23–25; xv. 3–8) must be regarded as samples of Paul's knowledge of the details of the life of Jesus. He appeals to the words of Jesus; he understands the character of Jesus; he knows what the message and mission of Jesus is."[4] The qualifications of Paul as an interpreter of Jesus challenge us at once in the verses[5] before us. I venture to say that he is the

[1] Cf. Warfield, "The Lord of Glory," for a full development of this argument.

[2] Gal. i. 18.

[3] Art. "Paul" in Hastings's D. C. G.

[4] Robertson, "Epochs in the Life of Paul," p. 89.

[5] 2 Cor. iv. 4–6.

supreme interpreter of Jesus Christ, he and John the Apostle. It is true that Paul's spiritual eyes had been blinded before the great light shone around him that day on the road to Damascus.[1] That light blinded the eyes of his body, but opened the eyes of his soul. "I could not see for the glory of that light." Yes, but he had seen the glory in the face of Jesus. "When his eyes were opened, he saw nothing"[2] but Jesus. That voice and that face followed him through life. In Damascus the scales fell from his eyes and the Holy Spirit came upon him and he was baptized, but he had already seen Jesus in the way.[3] That was his unbroken testimony that he had seen the Lord Jesus on the way to Damascus.[4] "I was not disobedient to the heavenly vision."[5] That transcendent experience was the *crux* upon which all of Paul's testimony turned. He never doubted its reality for one moment. Many persons had looked on the face of Jesus while in the flesh who did not understand Him. There was beyond doubt a wondrous fascination in the face of Jesus that no artist has succeeded in putting upon canvas. The pictures of Christ are either too effeminate or too crude.[6] No face has ever so haunted and

[1] Acts ix. 3; xxii. 6; xxvi. 13. [2] Acts ix. 8. [3] Acts ix. 17 f.
[4] Acts ix. 27; 1 Cor. xv. 8. [5] Acts xxvi. 19.
[6] Cf. Tissot, "The Life of Our Lord Jesus Christ" (1900), which is well done as a whole. See also "The Christ Face in Art."

baffled the greatest artists. This face was really human, but free from the taint of sin and disease. No spectres of the past looked through those eyes. No shadows of forbidden secrets flitted past. Pity, unutterable compassion, looked out of the depths of purity and unsullied strength. Untarnished truth looked out on a world of lies. The noblest impulses of man met the shock of hate and cnvy. The clear light of heaven's love gazed longingly at the suffering and the sinning. Those eyes could flash with terrific power upon hypocrites who used the livery of heaven to serve the devil in. Before His wrath men slunk away like cowed beasts, guilty and condemned. But the penitent and the contrite saw a new hope as they looked in the face of Jesus. There were some who could never forget the thrill of joy which came to their hearts as they gazed into His face. At moments they could be amazed at the struggling emotions in His countenance. There were three who beheld His majestic glory on the mount. But not all men could see all this in the face of Jesus. The rabbis were angered to desperation as they saw that calm and powerful face. Its very innocence enraged them. But Paul was a man gifted above his fellows. When once he did see Jesus Christ, he was in a position to see more than many other less gifted spirits. His soul was keyed to the highest tension as he looked into the face of Jesus. In his after study of that face he had the skill of a supreme artist. He never ceased looking. At first Paul had studied the picture of Jesus that he might see the secret of His power. "But, as he looked, there happened a strange thing—the picture crept into his soul. He had sought to find the secret of its power with the view of refuting it. He did find the secret of its power; but it refuted *him.* The gaze of anger was transmuted into a gaze of rapture."[1] Matheson calls Paul "the Illuminated" and it aptly describes the qualifications of Paul for his interpretation of Christ. "Remember, the Christ whom Paul first saw was the Christ in heaven. He never gazed upon the Man of Galilee. His earliest vision was the vision of a Jesus glorified. Not on the road to the Cross did Christ meet him; He came to him panoplied in heavenly splendour. What his inner eye beheld was the Christ of the future—a Christ of majesty, a Christ of power, a Christ who came clothed in the lightning and wreathed in the conqueror's robe. That was the first Christian image in Paul's soul. Is it wonderful that it should have been the first Christian image in his writings?"[2] The famous blind preacher has seen into the secret of Paul's soul.[3] It is interesting how

[1] Matheson, "Representative Men of the New Testament," p. 335.
[2] *Ibid.*, p. 343.
[3] Cf. also Matheson, "Spiritual Development of St. Paul."

fond Matheson was of pictures that he carried in his memory from the days before he lost his eyesight. He has seen with the eye of the soul more than many who had the sight of the eye.[1] Moses had once asked to look upon the glory of God. "Show me, I pray thee, Thy glory. . . . And He said, thou canst not see My face; for man shall not see Me and live. And Jehovah said, Behold there is a place by Me, and thou shalt stand upon the rock, and it shall come to pass, while My glory passeth by, that I will put thee in a cleft of the rock, and will cover thee with My hand until I have passed by: and I will take away My hand, and thou shalt see My back; but My face shall not be seen."[2] This is anthropomorphic, to be sure, but it marks the difference between the Old Covenant and the New. It is poetic imagery when Moses said: "For Thou, Jehovah, art seen face to face,"[3] though a great spiritual reality. God did manifest Himself in wonderful measure to Moses, but not as Paul saw God in the face of Christ. The Greek word for "face"[4] has also the idea of "person" as in 2 Corinthians i. 11; viii. 24. Paul several times speaks of the face of Christ.[5] It was more than a mere image to Paul, but he longed

[1] Cf. Matheson, "Studies of the Portrait of Christ." Two volumes.
[2] Ex. xxxiii. 18–23.
[3] Num. xiv. 14.
[4] 2 Cor. iv. 6.
[5] 1 Cor. xiii. 12; 2 Cor. ii. 10; 2 Thess. i. 9.

for the time when he would no longer see through a mirror as through a puzzling and baffling enigma, but would be able to look Jesus Christ in the eye again, "face to face."[1]

2. *The Image of God*

Paul expressly speaks of "Christ, who is the image of God."[2] By this term Paul means much more than moral likeness to God.[3] Man in his power bears the image and glory of God.[4] It is the destiny of believers to bear the image of the Son of God.[5] But in this passage Paul means a great deal more. He here presents not the idea of mere similarity,[6] but the representation and manifestation of God.[7] It is the divine nature and absolute moral excellence of Jesus that Paul has here in mind as in Colossians i. 15: "Who is the image of the invisible God, the first-born of all creation."[8] Paul had evidently come to see that Jesus Christ was worthy to be called God. Indeed, the correct text of Acts xx. 28, in Paul's address to the Ephesian elders, has "Church of God which He purchased with His own blood." So in Romans ix. 5 the most natural punctuation has "God blessed forever" in apposition to

[1] 1 Cor. xiii. 12.
[2] 2 Cor. iv. 4.
[3] Col. iii. 10; 1 Cor. xv. 49; Phil. iii. 21.
[4] 1 Cor. xi. 7.
[5] Rom. viii. 29; 2 Cor. iii. 18.
[6] Or likeness.
[7] Cf. Thayer's Lexicon.
[8] Cf. Heb. i. 3.

"Christ concerning the flesh, who is over all." Paul clearly taught the preëxistent state and glory of Jesus Christ in heaven.[1] Christ existed in the form of God and on an equality with God in heaven before His birth and humiliation.[2] Whatever the "Kenosis" means or does not mean, Paul is clear as to the essential deity of Christ in heaven. He had the form of God in heaven as He had the form of a servant on earth.[3] If He was a real man here, He was true God there. Paul grasped strongly the true deity of Jesus Christ into whose face he looked. It is not the "how," but the fact. Forsyth[4] puts the case of Paul as of all believers to-day when he says: "If we ask *how* Eternal Godhead could make the actual condition of human nature His own, we must answer, as I have already said, that we do not know. We cannot follow the steps of the process, or make a psychological sketch." Nor does Paul attempt it, though he is certain of the fact. It is reassuring at any rate to see how a great scientist like Sir Oliver Lodge[5] finds no objection on scientific grounds to the fact "that a Divine Spirit—that the Deity Himself, indeed—went through this process in order to make Himself known to man, and also in order fully to

[1] 2 Cor. viii. 9. [2] Phil. ii. 6. [3] Phil. ii. 7.
[4] "Person and Place of Jesus Christ," p. 320.
[5] "Jesus or Christ" (*Hibbert Journal Supplement* for 1909), p. 119.

realize the conditions and limitations of the free beings which, through evolution, had gradually been permitted to exist. . . . And this individualized and human aspect of the eternally Divine Spirit we know as Jesus of Nazareth, a man like ourselves, save that the glory of that lofty Spirit shone through the fleshly covering and preserved it from the load of sin which follows from inadequate knowledge, imperfect insight, animal ancestry, and alien will." In the face of this sure word from a really great scientist one need not be dismayed by the weak surrender of the deity of Jesus by modern theologians out of dread of "the category of supernaturalism." "One may question whether the first interpreters' speculations about Jesus can lay any stronger claim to finality than can their cosmology."[1] Dr. Case makes merry with the theologians who still believe that "God impinged upon the universe from without, He projected Himself into human history." But Sir Oliver Lodge, unlike Dr. Case, is not afraid of God in the face of Jesus Christ. We may never know how Christ is the image of God. Dr. Sanday has made a bold suggestion. He takes advantage of the new discussions concerning the subconscious self to suggest the possibility that the divine nature

[1] Prof. S. J. Case, of the Divinity School of the University of Chicago, *Biblical World*, Jan., 1911, p. 8.

of Jesus has its *locus* in this subliminal region of human nature.[1] He calls this notion "A Tentative Modern Christology." It is most assuredly attractive as over against the Chalcedonian conception of the Two Natures, but it is doubtful if after all it would not be a denial of the actual deity of Christ in spite of Dr. Sanday's express avowal of his own faith in the deity of Jesus Christ.[2] But it is more than likely that after all one will be merely playing with phrases which do not square with the actual facts. The consciousness may have no "planes" at all in a material sense and the conscious rational will is more important than the unconscious occasional impulses.[3] We shall probably have to continue to confess our ignorance of the ultimate facts concerning the Person of Christ. As a matter of fact, we do not understand either human nature in ourselves or divine nature in God. It is not surprising that we are somewhat helpless in grasping the idea of the combination of the two. Scientists like Lord Kelvin and Sir William Ramsay make no pretensions to expound the ultimate qualities of matter. Theologians may well be

[1] "Christologies Ancient and Modern," pp. 163 ff.

[2] Cf. Warfield, *Princeton Theological Review*, Jan., 1911, p. 172. For a sympathetic review of Dr. Sanday's idea see *The Interpreter* for Jan., 1911 (editorial).

[3] For an able *critique* of Dr. Sanday's position see "Theology and the Subconscious," by the Right Rev. C. F. D'Arcy, D. D., in the *Hibbert Journal* for Jan., 1911.

equally humble in the higher realm of spirit. But there is no doubt at all as to where Paul placed Jesus. "It is not putting it too strongly to say that He had for Paul the religious value of God. To suppose that Paul could have classified Him, and put Him in a series along with the other great men who have contributed to the spiritual elevation of the race, is to deride his sincerity and his passion."[1] It is just this conception of Jesus as God which has won for Him the adoration of men. "We might suppose that such an idea would grow faint and shadowy, that such an image would fade and melt away amid the rest of time's dreams. But as a matter of practical experience,

> "'That one face, far from vanish, rather grows,
> Or decomposes, but to recompose.'

All generations of believers have proved its strange, unearthly attraction, its enduring permanence, its mighty and miraculous power."[2]

3. *The Glory of God*

There was "the glory of God in the face of Jesus Christ."[3] Others besides Jesus have manifested the

[1] Denney, "Jesus and the Gospel," p. 27.
[2] Sir W. Robertson Nicoll in *The British Weekly*.
[3] 2 Cor. iv. 6.

glory of God. Paul[1] has just spoken of the fact that "the children of Israel could not look steadfastly upon the face of Moses for the glory of his face." This wonderful fact did not render Moses divine. For a careful argument showing the superiority of Jesus over Moses, as the Son is above the servant, see Hebrews iii. 1–6. He merely reflected the transcendent glory which he had been beholding. At the death of Elijah there came "a chariot of fire, and horses of fire which parted them asunder; and Elijah went up by a whirlwind into heaven."[2] But Elijah was not divine. The face of Stephen had looked like the face of an angel. He said: "Behold, I see the heavens opened, and the Son of man standing on the right hand of God."[3] In his exaltation Jesus is still "the Son of man." That is part of His glory.[4] There was a humiliation in the Incarnation of Christ. Paul in a marvellous way pictures the descent of Christ from the throne of God to the death of the Cross.[5] It is like coming down the long stairway. But the descent was just to open up the way to God. Jesus in His humanity was the way to God.[6] In His humanity He was able to give help to the seed of Abraham[7] and to make possible free communion with God. Jesus is the real Jacob's Ladder

[1] 2 Cor. iii. 7.
[2] 2 Kings ii. 11.
[3] Acts vi 15; vii. 56.
[4] Cf. Heb. iii. 1–10.
[5] Phil. ii. 5–9.
[6] John xiv. 6.
[7] Heb. ii. 16.

between heaven and earth.[1] Men can thus ascend upon the Son of man to heaven as angels descend upon Him. "But we behold Him who hath been made a little lower than the angels, *even* Jesus, because of the suffering of death crowned with glory and honour, that by the grace of God He should taste of death for every man."[2] There was a glory in Jesus in the days of His flesh. Peter if he wrote the Second Epistle (which I am glad to know is the view of Bigg[3]) has a vivid recollection of that wonderful night on the Mount of Transfiguration: "But we were eye-witnesses of His majesty. For He received from God the Father honour and glory, when there was borne such a voice to Him by the Majestic Glory, This is My beloved Son, in whom I am well pleased: and this voice we ourselves heard borne out of heaven, when we were with Him in the holy mount."[4] This transfiguration[5] was a temporary revelation of the glory which Jesus had with the Father before the Incarnation.[6] The time came when Jesus longed for a final restoration of that glory by His return to the Father. John adds his testimony to that of Peter: "We beheld His glory, glory as of the only begotten from the Father."[7] This took place after "the Word became flesh and

[1] John i. 51.
[2] Heb. ii. 9.
[3] "International and Crit. Commentary."
[4] 2 Pet. i. 16–18.
[5] Mark ix. 2.
[6] John xvii. 5.
[7] John i. 14.

dwelt among us" (tabernacled with us). Whether John is referring only to the Transfiguration of Jesus we do not know. He seems to include others in this witness. There were other times when there was a strange glory in the look of Jesus. As Jesus went up to Jerusalem the last time, full of thoughts of His death (as at the Transfiguration), we read: "And Jesus was going before them: and they were amazed; and they that followed were afraid."[1] But it was true of the whole life of Jesus that "He manifested His glory"[2] by His miracles. By the grave of Lazarus Jesus said to Martha: "Said I not unto thee that, if thou believedst, thou shouldst see the glory of God?"[3] It was true of Jesus, as it was not true of Moses, that He *was* and *is* the glory of God. "No man hath seen God at any time; the only begotten Son, who is in the bosom of the Father, He hath declared Him."[4] The best manuscripts here read "God only begotten." In His humanity Jesus has revealed the Father. The one who really sees Jesus has seen the Father.[5] Jesus is God's Word about Himself to men. He has made the full and final interpretation[6] of God to men. "He is the only window which opens out and gives the vision of that far-off land. I, for my part, believe that, if I

[1] Mark x. 32. [2] John ii. 11. [3] John xi. 40.
[4] John i. 18. [5] John xiv. 8 ff. [6] John i. 18.

might use such a metaphor, He is the Columbus of the New World."[1] This is Paul's conception of the glory of God in the face of Jesus Christ. "Christ on the throne was, if one may say so, a more immediate certainty to Paul, than Jesus on the banks of the lake, or even Jesus on the cross."[2]

4. *Christ Jesus as Lord*

This is the way Paul preached.[3] The words are carefully chosen. It is possible that Paul may have heard thus early of the incipient Gnosticism which later appeared in the Lycus Valley in Asia and which is combated in Colossians[4] and Ephesians. But that is hardly probable, though Paul had recently come from Ephesus. These Gnostics were of two types in their attitude towards the Person of Christ. The Docetic Gnostics denied the actual humanity of Christ. He merely seemed to be a man. The Cerinthian Gnostics made a sharp distinction between the man Jesus and the Christ (an *æon* or emanation of God which came upon Jesus at His baptism and left Him before His death on the Cross). The language of Paul here at any rate contravenes both of these theories, especially the Cerinthian. He identi-

[1] Maclaren, "Expositions of Holy Scripture," 2 Corinthians, p. 328.

[2] Denney, 2 Corinthians, p. 154.

[3] 2 Cor. iv. 5.

[4] So Lightfoot. Hort, "Judaistic Christianity," fails to see any reference to Gnosticism.

fies the one personality whom he designates "Christ Jesus" as also "Lord." He was the man Jesus, the Messiah (Christ), the Lord of glory. There has been a curious swinging of the pendulum among certain theologians through the ages concerning the person of Christ. The Ebionites denied the deity of Jesus. The Docetic Gnostics rejected His humanity. Paul recognized both as true of Christ Jesus. He is to Paul the God-man. Is this reality or merely Paul's interpretation? Paul did not originate this interpretation. The other apostles had so understood Jesus. Hear Peter on the Day of Pentecost: "Let all the house of Israel know assuredly that God hath made Him both Lord and Christ, this Jesus whom ye crucified."[1] If one begin with the earliest known sources of the life of Christ according to modern criticism, either Q (the Logia of Matthew) or Mark's Gospel, he will find Jesus Christ the Lord of glory there.[2] The Christ of the Synoptic Gospels, of Paul, of John, of Hebrews, of Peter, of James, of the Apocalypse is one and the same; Jesus Christ the same yesterday and to-day and forever.[3] The various writers of the New Testament approach the

[1] Acts ii. 36.
[2] Cf. Mullins, "The Modern Issue as to the Person of Christ," *Review and Expositor*, Jan., 1911, pp. 14ff.
[3] See this argument worked out with great ability and detail by Warfield, "The Lord of Glory"; Denney, "Jesus and the Gospel"; Selbie, "Aspects of Christ." Biblical Theology, accenting the

study of Jesus from different angles, but each comes to the same point in fact. It is a lame conclusion to which Schweitzer comes in his "Quest of the Historical Jesus." After long rambles through the mazes of conflicting critical theories he says: "He comes to us as One unknown, without a name, as of old, by the lake-side, He came to those men who knew Him not."[1] None are so blind as those who will not see. Men come to Christ to-day, as of old, with their prejudices and their philosophy and cannot see His glory because of the fog around their own heads. The sun shines brightly for all who can get out of the fog. The very "greatness of Christ"[2] makes critical interpretation difficult and in a sense impossible. It is hard to look straight at the sun. But the sun shines on regardless of the changing theories about light and the spots in the sun. "The Life of Christ in Recent Research"[3] is an interesting topic, as is "The Place of Christ in Modern Theology."[4] We must use freely and frankly our reason and all light from every source for the interpretation of Jesus Christ. We have nothing to fear. Evolution "has set Christ in a new light. Confined within

variations in the New Testament, and criticism of the sources have thus combined greatly to strengthen the argument for the truth of Paul's view of Jesus.

[1] P. 401.

[2] Forsyth, "Person and Place of Jesus Christ," pp. 63 ff.

[3] Sanday.

[4] Fairbairn.

human limits, He is the stultification of the calculations of evolutionists, viewed as our moral natures direct us to view Him, He is the goal and crown of the evolutionary process in the history of man."[1] It is a curious controversy that has arisen around the phrase "Jesus or Christ" and that appears in *The Hibbert Journal Supplement*.[2] But at any rate one can get here all sides of the problem. The point with Rev. R. Roberts, who started the discussion, is that Jesus as an historical character is one thing, the Christ of tradition quite another. It is assumed that criticism has disposed of the connection between Jesus and Christ. Criticism has done nothing of the kind. Some critics deny the historicity of Jesus altogether. In Germany there is a controversy over the historical reality of Jesus.[3] Other critics admit the reality of Jesus, and make Christ a matter of faith. Others reject the Christ entirely and see only a good man named Jesus who is our example today. Others admit the existence of Jesus, and, like Nietzsche, rail at Him as the curse of the race by reason of the limitations on self-indulgence which He has imposed on the "super-man." But most of the ablest critics in the world still joyfully see in Jesus

[1] G. A. Johnston Ross, "Religionist and Scientist" in "Religion and the Modern World," p. 14.

[2] For 1909.

[3] Cf. *Biblische Zeitschrift*, 1910, S. 415–17, for bibliography of this discussion; also *American Journal of Theology*, Jan., 1911.

Christ what Paul saw, the man Christ Jesus as the Lord of glory, Son of God and Son of Man. "Therefore, not 'away from Paul and back to Jesus,' but rather as one[1] of his recent apologists puts it, 'Back through Paul to Jesus and to God.'"[2] To Paul Jesus was and is Lord of life, the very power of God at work among men.[3] When *Ecce Homo* first appeared many feared to look at this bold and brilliant picture of the earthly life of Jesus. But now we can come back from the fuller study of "the days of His flesh" to a richer knowledge of His heavenly glory. We see no conflict between the "Christ of History and Experience."[4] But one must have the experience before he is really qualified to study the history. The alternative "Jesus or Christ" exists only for those who have never learned by experience "what is the riches of the glory of this mystery among the Gentiles, which is Christ in you, the hope of glory."[5] To Paul Christ is the mystery of God,[6] "for in Him dwelleth all the fullness of the Godhead bodily."[7]

[1] A. Meyer, *Jesus oder Paulus*, S. 104.
[2] George Milligan, "Paulinism and the Religion of Jesus" in "Religion and the Modern World," p. 253.
[3] Col. i. 15–17; cf. Selbie, "Aspects of Christ," p. 88.
[4] Forrest. [5] Col. i. 27. [6] Col. ii. 2.
[7] Col. ii. 9. "The Christ of To-day" (G. Campbell Morgan) is the Christ of Paul.

5. *The Gospel of the Glory of Christ*

This is Paul's Christology: "The light of the Gospel of the glory of Christ."[1] He speaks twice in Romans[2] of "My Gospel." He means by that phrase his interpretation of Christ, "the Gospel of Christ."[3] Paul had a definite message about Jesus to preach to men. It is seen in its fullest expression in the Epistle to the Romans, but it is found with more or less fullness in all his writings. There is little excuse for any man, minister or not, to take the time and attention of others, if he has not made up his mind about Jesus Christ. No message of doubt or negation will benefit the soul sick with sin and battling with temptation. Paul felt that he had the right to speak just because of his actual knowledge of Jesus Christ who had revealed Himself in him.[4] He knew the Gospel of Christ.[5] Paul felt that a high and holy trust was given to him. He told Timothy of "the Gospel of the glory of the blessed God which was committed to my trust."[6] "To catch but a passing vision of the glory of God is to burn forever afterwards with a zeal to make it known."[7] No one could deceive him with a different message. He has only irony for those who put up with "another

[1] 2 Cor. iv. 4; cf. iv. 6.
[2] Rom. ii. 16; xvi. 25.
[3] Rom. xv. 19.
[4] Gal. i. 16.
[5] Gal. i. 6–10.
[6] 2 Tim. i. 11; cf. Gal. ii. 7.
[7] Greenough, "The Mind of Christ in St. Paul," p. 14.

Jesus," "a different spirit," "a different Gospel."[1] It is only about the most tremendous things in life that Paul has such a strong word. He is the exponent of freedom for the Gentile Christians from the bondage of Judaism. "For freedom did Christ set us free."[2] But liberty is not license. To give up Christ is to give up liberty and have either the slavery of license or the bondage of the letter. Paul is here an example for the modern minister in the firm grasp of the essential truth in Christ with the utmost liberality in all other matters. The preacher to-day has to sail between the Scylla of traditionalism and the Charybdis of radicalism. But Paul kept his eye on Christ. There is no better interpreter of Jesus Christ than Paul.[3] He grew in his apprehension of Christ,[4] as can be seen by reading his Epistles in probable chronological order.[5] But he never got away from his early conception of Jesus as the Redeemer and of salvation by grace through faith.[6] There is a distinct "mental growth"[7] perceptible in Paul as he

[1] 2 Cor. xi. 4. [2] Gal. v. 1.

[3] See DuBose, "The Gospel According to St. Paul"; Bruce, "St. Paul's Conception of Christianity"; Somerville, "St. Paul's Conception of Christ"; Stevens, "Pauline Theology"; Dykes, "The Gospel According to St. Paul"; Anonymous, "The Fifth Gospel, The Pauline Interpretation."

[4] See Matheson, "Spiritual Development of St. Paul"; Sabatier, "The Apostle Paul."

[5] Robertson, "Students' Chronological New Testament."

[6] Acts xiii. 38 f.

[7] Fairbairn, "Studies in Religion and Theology," p. 535.

grapples with the greatest questions ever brought before the human mind. He became the greatest intellectual expounder of Christ in all history. He is that to-day. He had "the light of the Gospel of the glory of Christ, who is the image of God."[1] He was able "to give the light of the knowledge of the glory of God in the face of Jesus Christ."[2] The "light"[3] was an illumination of Paul's own inner man. It filled the whole horizon of his life.

6. *Who Shined in Our Hearts*

With Paul this was the beginning of everything when God shone in his heart. He has in the words, "Light shall shine out of darkness,"[4] a reference to Genesis i. 3.[5] "It is the proclamation of a second *Fiat Lux* in the hearts of men."[6] Jesus was the Light of the world in the cosmic creative sense in the beginning.[7] "The life was the light of men. And the light shineth in the darkness; and the darkness overcame it not."[8] The darkness could not put out the Light in the terrific conflict that ensued. But men became so used to the darkness that they could not see when the light came. "I am come a light into the world;"[9] "I am the light of the world."[10] "And

[1] 2 Cor. iv. 4.
[2] 2 Cor. iv. 6.
[3] The word occurs nowhere else in the New Testament.
[4] 2 Cor. iv. 6.
[5] Cf. Ps. xcii. 4.
[6] Bernard, *in loco.*
[7] Cf. John i. 3 f.; Col. i. 16 f.
[8] John i. 4 f.; cf. John xii. 35.
[9] John xii. 46.
[10] John viii. 12.

this is the judgment, that the light is come into the world, and men loved the darkness rather than the light, for their works were evil."[1] "Look therefore whether the light that is in thee be not darkness."[2] Isaiah had foreseen the glory of Christ and that, when He came, men's eyes would be blinded so that they could not see the light.[3] Paul has lived to see the sad fulfillment of this prophecy, "The god of this world hath blinded the minds of the unbelieving, that the light of the Gospel of the glory of Christ, who is the image of God, should not dawn upon them."[4] It was like daybreak[5] in any heart when God let the Light in the face of Jesus shine in. The word of prophecy was well in its place. It was like "a lamp shining in a dark place."[6] It is a squalid,[7] dirty, dark place. In a dungeon a lamp is a blessing of untold comfort. But the lamp was of special use only "until the day dawn, and the day-star arise in your hearts."[8] The "light-bringing" star has arisen in our hearts. It is daybreak in our souls. We no longer need the lamp. God "shined in our hearts."[9] This is the fundamental fact with Paul, as with all disciples of Jesus. "In that face which flashed upon

[1] John iii. 19.
[2] Luke xii. 35.
[3] John xii. 40 f.; Isa. vi. 10.
[4] 2 Cor. iv. 4.
[5] Cf. Rev. xxi. 21.
[6] 2 Peter i. 19.
[7] Here only in the New Testament.
[8] Day-star here only in the New Testament.
[9] Cf. Lietzmann, *Handbuch zum N. T.*, 2 Kor., S. 182.

him by Damascus twenty years before, he had seen, and always saw, all that man could see of the invisible God. It represented for him, and all to whom he preached, the Sovereignty and the Redeeming Love of God, as completely as man could understand them."[1] He could not indeed see for the glory of that light which made the noonday sun dim by comparison.[2] But henceforth he could see naught else but the glory in the face of Jesus. This to him was the sheet-anchor of his faith, hope, theology, life. "I know Him whom I have believed."[3] Others might or might not know Jesus Christ. That did not affect Paul in the least. He is now crucified with Christ. "And it is no longer I that live, but Christ liveth in me."[4] The key-word of Paul's life is "in Christ." Into this mystic phrase Paul pours all the content of his life and thought about Christ.[5] Paul grounds his apologetic in his own experience. That is scientific and modern as well, in perfect harmony with the evolutionary principle. It is no longer possible to ridicule Christian experience as something abnormal and distorted. William James[6] did a great service to the world in showing the scien-

[1] Denney, 2 Corinthians, p. 153. [2] Acts xxii. 11; xxvi. 13.
[3] 2 Tim. i. 12. [4] Gal. ii. 20.
[5] Cf. Campbell, "Paul the Mystic"; Deissmann, "Die Neutestamentliche Formel in Christo."
[6] "Varieties in Religious Experience."

tific aspect of religious experience. With Paul it was an illumination[1] which shed light into the secret places of his heart and life. Christ is the true light who gives all the real light that any man has.[2] Those who had once for all[3] been enlightened could never forget that experience and were ready to endure much conflict.[4] Jesus had brought to light life and immortality through the Gospel for all those who had the eyes of their hearts enlightened.[5] The image is a favourite one in the New Testament. John pictures heaven as needing no sun nor moon, "for the glory of God did lighten it, and the lamp thereof is the Lamb."[6] The dynamic of the Cross is central in Paul's mind.[7] He does not mean that his own case is peculiar in this respect. The rather, he argues that, if God could save him through Christ, no one need despair.[8] It is just because Jesus can save the worst of men that the preacher has the heart and hope to go on with his work. The self-conscious religionist often rejects Christ when the vilest sinners joyfully repent and put the "righteous" to shame.[9] "The adequacy of the Christian redemp-

[1] Cf. Eph. i. 18. [2] John i. 9. [3] Heb. vi. 4.
[4] Heb. vi. 32.
[5] 2 Tim. i. 10; Eph. i. 18. [6] Rev. xxi. 23; xxii. 5.
[7] Cf. Clow, "The Cross and Christian Experience."
[8] Cf. 2 Tim. i. 14–16.
[9] Luke v. 30 f. Cf. Begbie, "Twice-born Men," and "Souls in Action."

tion lies in its power to meet this primal need by removing the misery and guilt of sin."[1]

7. *For Jesus' Sake*

"For we preach not ourselves."[2] That is the poorest theme ever taken by a preacher, himself. It is bad homiletics as well as bad religion when a preacher is full of himself, for he is sure to reveal it in numberless ways. Paul is ironical towards the Judaizers in Corinth who "commend themselves: but they themselves, measuring themselves by themselves, and comparing themselves with themselves, are without understanding."[3] They are the standard and are always right. They always come up to the standard, viz., themselves. Paul here evidently has them in mind. They *do* preach themselves. It is probably true that most ecclesiastical schisms have had their origin in personal jealousies and bickerings. And yet while "Christ Jesus as Lord" is the theme of Paul's preaching, he does in one sense preach himself—"and ourselves as your servants for Jesus' sake."[4] He was the slave of Christ and the slave[5] of his brethren. It was much for this proud-spirited man so to describe himself. But this is the spirit of

[1] "Final Christianity," by D. MacFadyen, in "Mansfield College Essays," p. 211.
[2] 2 Cor. iv. 5. [3] 2 Cor. x. 12. [4] 2 Cor. iv. 5. [5] Bond-slave.

Jesus, service to others.[1] It was for this purpose that the light had come into his own heart "to give the light of the knowledge of the glory of God in the face of Jesus Christ."[2] He had faced Christ and must reflect the glory of that Face to others in darkness. He was to pass on the light. Paul knew "The Passion for Souls"[3] "for Jesus' Sake." Matheson describes the Twelve Apostles of Jesus as "His league of pity."[4] That is a fit characterization of ministers of Christ. The hunger of the heart is for Christ. Men know it after they have found Him. The need of the preacher is just this. He has his vision of the Face of Christ. He must turn the man without the vision to Christ. The Greeks came to Philip with a pathetic inquiry: "Sir, we would see Jesus."[5] Strange to say Philip did not introduce them to Jesus. He went instead to Andrew. Together they could not unravel the problem and brought it to Jesus. It touched the heart of Christ in the centre. The Cross came before His mind at once. Thus alone would Gentiles be able to come to Him, for thus would the middle wall of partition between Jew and Gentile and both and God be broken down.[6] The modern minister stands beside the matchless portrait of Jesus Christ and hears the same cry from the

[1] Matt. xx. 28. [2] 2 Cor. iv. 6. [3] J. H. Jowett.
[4] "Studies of the Portrait of Christ," Vol. II, p. 83.
[5] John xii. 21. [6] Eph. ii.

masses: "Sir, we would see Jesus." It is not enough just to be willing "to speak a gude word for Jesus Christ," though that is much. One must be able to interpret that Picture to modern men. But first he must himself really see the Face of Christ, else his talk is sounding brass and tinkling cymbal. Paul has soared high. "No one ever soared so high on borrowed wings."[1]

[1] Denney, "Jesus and the Gospel," p. 38.

IV

WITH OPEN FACE—THE PREACHER'S PRIVILEGE

(*2 Cor. iii. 17–iv. 4*)

"We all, with unveiled face, beholding as in a glass the glory of the Lord."

—*2 Cor. iii. 18.*

IV

WITH OPEN FACE—THE PREACHER'S PRIVILEGE

THE "open face" is really the "unveiled face."[1] It is in sharp contrast with Moses who put a veil over his face. By "we all" Paul means all Christians, though the argument is specifically applied to ministers of the Gospel: "Therefore seeing we have this ministry."[2] It is the privilege of all believers; it is preëminently true of the preacher, not because of office or rank, but because of necessity he is constantly brought face to face with God in Christ. The minister has his "Holy of Holies" with Christ.

1. *Where the Spirit of the Lord Is*

One naturally thinks of a church by the use of this phrase.[3] Some churches are narrow and reactionary, tied to mere tradition. But Paul seems here to have in mind the minister himself. The man into whose heart the Spirit of the Lord has come has freedom from fear that the glory will die away as

[1] There is thus a direct reference to iii. 7, 13.

[2] 2 Cor. iv. 1.

[3] 2 Cor. iii. 17.

with Moses. He is emancipated from anxiety that the people will not give him a proper degree of honour. He is not concerned about the amount of recognition which is accorded him at public functions. He has liberty, as Christ's freeman, from the bondage of the letter (condemnation, death). His is a ministry of the Spirit because the Spirit of the Lord has command of his heart and life. The Spirit-filled minister is empty of fear. There is no veil upon his face. Hence he has uninterrupted fellowship with Jesus and with the people. He is able to see "the light of the knowledge of the glory of God in the face of Jesus Christ" as well as to "give" it to others. Dr. Sanday [1] is patient with the Ritschlian type of "reduced Christianity" since it is that much positive gain over mere negation. Ritschlianism is proudly independent of historical facts and professes content with giving Jesus the "worth" of God as a practical matter. He very probably was not God in any metaphysical ontological sense according to this view, but one may find comfort in treating Him so. That is at bottom a make-believe doctrine and unworthy of the great issue involved.[2] The concession of Dr. Sanday about the subliminal self as the *locus* of the divine nature of Jesus is already urged as

[1] "Christologies, Ancient and Modern."
[2] Cf. Orr, "Ritschlianism."

making Dr. Sanday more of a Ritschlian than he thinks,[1] since it does not demand the Virgin Birth. But Paul does not here mean the license of a half-hearted Christianity. That is after all the bondage of doubt and fear. It is love that makes us really free to do right. "Love makes the choice easy. Love makes the face of duty beautiful. Love makes it sweet to keep up with Christ. Love makes the service of goodness freedom."[2] This liberty in service is to Paul the distinguishing feature of Christianity.[3] He has no notion of giving it up "because of the false brethren privily brought in, who came in privily to spy out our liberty which we have in Christ Jesus, that they may bring us into bondage."[4] There are always on hand some men who feel called to slip a noose on the neck of God's freemen, but Paul would wear no man's yoke but that of Christ. "If therefore the Son shall make you free, ye shall be free indeed."[5] Jesus put it also thus: "Ye shall know the truth and the truth shall make you free."[6] The only real emancipation is in the truth, and Jesus is the truth. Paul is no blind obscurantist. He glories in his freedom from the fetters of Pharisaism. In Christ he faces the whole world and all fact and

[1] Shailer Matthews, *American Journal of Theology*, Jan., 1910, p. 136.

[2] Greenough, "The Mind of Christ in St. Paul," p. 216.

[3] *Ibid.*, p. 39. [4] Gal. ii. 4. [5] John viii. 36. [6] John viii. 32.

truth with open eye and eager heart. No one has anything like the liberty of the man whose mind is opened by the Spirit of Christ. Some Christians, some ministers, are in truth mere traditionalists, obscurantists afraid of the light. But that is not what should be nor what is meant to be by the Spirit of Christ. There are reactionaries in medicine, science, law, business, every calling of life. Certainly the man who refuses to face all the facts of the spiritual life in Christ is not free. Such freedom is only possible where the Spirit of the Lord is. "The Lord is the Spirit" hardly means simple identification of Jesus and the Spirit. The thought is not so simple as that. It is rather Christ manifesting Himself through His Spirit who is the great teacher and interpreter of Christ to men. The minister who is Christ's slave is the real freeman, free to look God and man full in the face with open heart and upright purpose. The Christian minister is to expound principles, not mere rules. There is the utmost frankness in his attitude and life. The veil has been taken away from his face. The people are not afraid to come close to him as they were with Moses.[2] The Christian ministry is thus[3] a "spiritual" ministry, a "life-giving" ministry, a "bold" ministry. "Ours should be a

[1] 2 Cor. iii. 16. [2] Ex. xxxiv. 30.
[3] F. W. Robertson, "Life and Letters," etc., p. 624 f.

ministry whose words are not compacted of baldness, but boldness; whose very life is outspokenness, and free fearlessness; a ministry which has no concealment, no reserve; which scorns to take a *via media* because it is safe in the eyes of the world; which shrinks from the weakness of mere cautiousness, but which exults even in failure, if the truth has been spoken, with a joyful confidence. For a man who sees into the heart of things speaks out not timidly, nor superstitiously, but with a brow unveiled, and with a speech as free as his spirit: 'The truth has made him free.'"[1] Paul is so free from narrowness and jealousy that he rejoices when Christ is preached even though the motive may be envy of Paul (Phil. i. 17 f.) or mere pretense.

2. *Transformation*

This freedom of the Christian is no mere theory with Paul. He can proudly appeal to the experience of all real disciples, preachers and all, in contrast to the Jews under the Mosaic dispensation. "We all, with unveiled face, are transformed into the same image."[2] There is doubt whether here Paul means

[1] F. W. Robertson, "Life and Letters," etc., p. 675. Cf. Wordsworth:

> "While with an eye made quiet by the power
> Of harmony and the deep power of joy
> We see into the life of things."

[2] 2 Cor. iii. 18.

"beholding in a mirror" or "reflecting as a mirror."[1] The analogy of 1 Corinthians xiii. 12: "For now we see in a mirror, darkly; but then face to face" argues for "beholding."[2] It is true that we shall not look Christ fully in the face till we meet Him in glory when we shall see Him as He is.[3] But even Moses had no veil on his face as he beheld the glory of God and it can hardly be a mere indirect look at Christ that Paul has in mind. He expressly mentions "the face of Jesus Christ." It is doubtless true, however, that this word is to be thus translated here, since Paul in this context has both ideas in mind. All believers have free access to the Face of Jesus Christ, the Glory and Image of God. It is no mere contemplation of the moral beauty of Jesus of Nazareth that fills the vision of Paul. No mere historical study of the facts in the earthly life of Jesus will suffice to work this transformation in the heart and life. The transformation is wrought by the Spirit of God in the heart that, free from the veil, is in actual touch with Christ the Lord of glory.[4] There is contemplation of the glory of Christ, transformation into the glory of Christ, final assimilation

[1] Only here in the New Testament.

[2] So in Philo, *Leg. All.* iii. 33, a comment on Ex. xxxiii. 18. The active means to mirror or reflect, while the middle voice, as here, means to behold in a mirror. Cf. Bernard, *in loco;* Meyer, *in loco;* Bachmann, *in loco*, for discussion of the details.

[3] 1 John iii. 2.

[4] Denney, 2 Corinthians, p. 140 f.

into the glory of Christ.[1] The word for "transformation"[2] is a remarkable one. It is the word used of the glory of Christ at the Transfiguration. It is then a transfiguration which we are undergoing. It is the present tense and the act is represented as a process. The new life in Christ begins with a look as the heart turns to Him. It grows by looking also, steadily bathing in the glory of the Sun of righteousness. "In spiritual sight, the soul which beholds is a mirror."[3] What seems like an impossibility vanishes when we consider that it is the glory of God in Christ that Paul has in mind and that the seeing takes place by the eye of faith, the eye of the soul.[4] It is true that, as contrasted with the final vision of Christ, we now see through a mirror darkly. "But nothing intervenes between my Lord and me, when I love and trust."[5] The reality of this spiritual perception of Christ is witnessed by millions of believers in all the ages since Paul wrote these words. To many Jesus Christ is the most real person in the universe. "The whole tendency of modern thought is to emphasize the importance of personality. Personality is the predominant factor in history and in

[1] Maclaren, "Expositions of Holy Scripture," *in loco.*
[2] Cf. Matt. xvii. 2.
[3] Maclaren, "Expositions of Holy Scripture," *in loco.*
[4] *Ibid.*
[5] *Ibid.*

life."[1] Jesus had definitely laid hold on[2] Paul. Henceforth to "gain Christ," to "know Him," to learn "the excellency of the knowledge of Christ Jesus my Lord," all this was the "one thing" which consumed his soul, the single goal of his life-ambition.[3] A minister, to whom this experience of Christ is unknown, cannot be considered qualified to tell men about Jesus. He must himself be transfigured by the Spirit of Christ, have the Spirit of Christ in him,[4] if he hopes to see others transfigured by his life and words. This spiritual appropriation is the first result of contact with Christ. This is to "eat"[5] Christ, to "see" the Face of Christ, to "behold" His glory, to become like Him, even as Moses had the glory of God upon him. There is no magic about it. There is mysticism, indeed, for religion is mysticism. It is the vital touch of the human spirit by the Spirit of Christ. Thus the vision of Christ comes to the soul. Thus the vision is continued. The Gospels, the Acts, the Epistles, the Apocalypse, the work of Christ in the hearts of men, the work of Christ in our own hearts—these are all mirrors to help us see the glory of Christ.[6]

3. *Reflection*

As we have already seen, there is no doubt that

[1] Richard Brook, *The Interpreter*, Jan., 1911, art., "The Living Christ and the Christian Life." [2] Phil. iii. 12. [3] Phil. iii. 8–14.
[4] Rom. viii. 9. [5] John vi. 57. [6] Cf. Bachmann, *in loco*.

this context calls for "reflecting as a mirror the glory of the Lord" as an implied idea however Paul meant the precise word here employed. Stanley[1] holds that "Christians having, like Moses, received in their lives the reflected glory of the divine presence, as Moses received it on his countenance, are unlike Moses in that they have no fear, such as his, of its vanishing away, but are confident of its continuing to shine in them with increasing lustre." The Christian puts on no veil for he has nothing to conceal. His life is an open book to the world. He does not, indeed, claim that his life is perfect, but that there is at least a reflection, however dim, of the real spirit and power of Christ, his Lord. "There is no reflection of the light without a previous reception of the light. In bodily sight, the eye is a mirror, and there is no sight without an image of the thing perceived being formed in the perceiving eye."[2] Chrysostom compares the influence of the light of Christ on us to polished silver lying in the sunshine and sending back the rays which strike it.[3] He says, "We not only look upon the glory of God, but also catch thence a kind of radiance."[4] But, at any rate, reflection is an inevitable result of transformation.[5]

[1] 2 Corinthians, *in loco.*
[2] Maclaren, "Expositions of Holy Scripture," *in loco.*
[3] Denney, 2 Corinthians, *in loco.* [4] Hom. VII on 2 Cor.
[5] Denney, *in loco.*

If we behold the glory of the Lord, we are transformed into the image of what we behold. If we are transformed, we reflect that image. There is no veil to prevent the glory from being seen, if only the glory is there to be seen. It is a severe test to which the Apostle John calls us when he says: "He that saith he abideth in Him ought himself also to walk even as He walked."[1] But it is the test to which we have to submit. In particular, ministers of the Gospel cannot refuse to be held up to the light which they hold forth to others. The world does not demand absolute perfection of us. It does require sincerity and steady going on in spite of frequent stumblings. "Even if a man be overtaken in a fault, ye which are spiritual, restore such an one in a spirit of meekness; looking to thyself lest thou also be tempted."[2] Jesus singled out Peter for a special message[3] after His resurrection and a special appearance. Paul was glad in the end to rejoice in the recovery of usefulness by John Mark who had once deserted the work.[4] It was part of Paul's call "to open their eyes, and to turn them from darkness to light."[5] "It is a critical moment in the history of the soul when the eyes are opened. Everything depends on whether the next step is taken. Men's

[1] 1 John ii. 6. [2] Gal. vi. 1. [3] Mark xvi. 7.
[4] Acts xv. 38; 2 Tim. iv. 11. [5] Acts xxvi. 18.

eyes are often opened, and yet they do not turn from darkness to light. Who among us has not seen, as in a flash of light, the error of his ways, and has loathed himself, and had the self-abasing cry on his lips, and yet has turned to darkness again and plunged even more recklessly into evil? It is possible for a man to know the misery of wrong-doing, and to describe it with such a horror of it as to rouse others to forsake it, and yet because he loves darkness better than light to continue to do the deeds of evil."[1] There is much to humble any man who stands in the white light of Christ's presence. And then to know that men will see Christ or not according as He is reflected in our own conduct! But here is just the appeal to the best and highest in us. Peter and John were both with Jesus at His trial; John in the court room, Peter with the rabble denying Him with oaths and curses. But both afterwards showed courage and were recognized as having been with Christ.[2] John had the courage of consistency, Peter that of recovery. It has not been easy for Christ to impart to men His passion for humanity,[3] but He has done it and His kingdom goes on with the momentum of His Spirit. One thing is certain. It does only harm to affect likeness to Christ which we

[1] Clow, "The Cross in Christian Experience," pp. 259 f.
[2] Acts iv. 13, 20.
[3] Carver, "Missions and Modern Thought," p. 283.

do not possess. Hypocrisy is the sin which called forth the most terrible words uttered by Jesus.[1] The only way to reflect the glory of God in Christ is to be like Him. There is no need of a veil so long as we continue to behold the face of Christ. If we lose sight of His face and glory, no veil can hide our failure from men. "Ye are the light of the world," says Jesus. "Even so let your light shine before men."

4. *Perseverance*

"We faint not,"[2] says Paul. He still has before him "the cry of human insufficiency"[3] uttered in Corinthians ii. 16. He is still answering it in a triumphant tone. The Greek manuscripts vary here in the word for "faint." The best attested word[4] occurs also in verse sixteen and in Galatians vi. 9: "And let us not be weary in well-doing: for in due season we shall reap, if we faint not." There are difficulties enough in a ministry with all this transcendent glory to test the stoutest heart. When Paul is a prisoner in Rome he actually has to cheer the Christians who have grown discouraged by reason of his troubles: "Wherefore I ask that you faint not at my tribulations for you."[5] Paul reminds Timothy that God

[1] Matt. xxiii.
[2] 2 Cor. iv. 1.
[3] Greenough, "The Mind of Christ in St. Paul," p. 293.
[4] Cf. our "giving in" to evil.
[5] Eph. iii. 13.

had given us a spirit of power, not of cowardly fear.[1] He did this when he was an old preacher in prison and facing certain death while Timothy was young and at work. Timothy was the one who needed to be exhorted to endure hardship as a good soldier of Christ." [2] Etymologically the word for "faint" could mean to "abandon one's self to badness," but no examples of just this sense occur. But it is used for cowardly surrender. Often the dead pull of things is hard to overcome. It is easy just to give up and quit. Just to stick to one's task and go on is the hard thing when the first flush of the romance is over. John Mark "went not to the work" [3] when he faced at Perga the perils of rivers and perils of robbers that confronted Paul and Barnabas. John Mark went home to Jerusalem. Paul and Barnabas conquered a kingdom for Christ. Courage in the ministry comes from the clear vision of Christ and the world's need of Him. "Therefore seeing we have this ministry," [4] says Paul; this ministry of spiritual freedom and power. It is the muck-raker who does not see the angels. Elisha's servant grew afraid at Dothan when he saw the host with horses and chariots: "Alas, my master! how shall we do? And he answered, Fear not: for they that are with

[1] 2 Tim. i. 7. [2] 2 Tim. ii. 1–13. [3] Acts xv. 36.

[4] 2 Cor. iv. 1. He applies here all the argument about the superiority of the ministry of the New Covenant to that of the Old.

us are more than they that be with them. And Elisha prayed, and said, Lord, I pray Thee, open his eyes, that he may see. And the Lord opened the eyes of the young man; and he saw: and, behold, the mountain was full of horses and chariots of fire round about Elisha."[1] Oh, for the vision of the power of Christ in the midst of the battle. Paul had this vision, "even as we obtained mercy."[2] He never ceases to rejoice in that.[3] The true leader sounds the bugle note of victory if the lines begin to waver. There is no retreat for Paul, but the onward march. The ground of Paul's cheer is not in the marks of appreciation which he received from men. It springs from the fresh gaze into the face of Jesus. Look at Jesus and you will go on with your task. "And let us not be weary in well-doing: for in due season we shall reap, if we faint not."

In Chapter I occurs a letter from a minister who gave up the ministry. Here is a reply in the same journal:

"DEAR WILLIAM: I have not a doubt that all your causes of discouragement are real, and hard to bear; but I am sorry you are leaving the pastorate. You have been a long time on your present field. Can you not try another one? New people, and different conditions, will doubtless cheer you and give you a fresh grip.

[1] 2 Kings vii. 15-17.

[2] 2 Cor. iv. 1.

[3] 2 Cor. vii. 25; 1 Tim. i. 13, 16.

"Of course, if you have become convinced that God never called you to the ministry, that is an end of the matter, and ought to be. But if it is a matter of disappointment, suffering, and fear of the future, you must remember that Christian ministers to-day are the successors of the prophets. The prophet is the man of larger vision than the people, the man who seeks to redeem the people to his own higher standards, the man who pleads with God for the people and asks that He be patient with their dullness and forgive their sins. The minister who stands in this relation to the people must ever bear in his heart something of disappointment and suffering.

"No Christian minister can be free from the redemptive principle, that the chastisement of the people's peace is upon him, and with his stripes they are healed. In different centuries this principle finds expression in different forms. Of the ancient prophets, the Lord said, 'Which of them did your fathers not stone?' Of the modern prophets it might with equal pertinency be inquired, 'To which of them do your churches pay salaries regularly, and in sufficient amount?' I confess, William, that for myself, I prefer the latter alternative.

"But what is more, the minister of Christ must not forget the experiences of his Lord, and must be ready, when necessary, to undergo like experiences. At Capernaum on one occasion, all but the twelve left the Saviour, and to these He said, 'Will ye also go away?' That is, He was left with a 'few faithful ones.' But these few became the salt of the earth, just as before them the 'remnant' was the salt of Israel. The words, 'The servant is not above his master,' had scarcely fallen from the lips of Christ ere He was crucified, and crucified by religious people. For myself, William, I would rather endure any modern crucifixion than the crucifixion that was meted out to my Master. I would rather endure any hardships which are incident to the modern ministry, than to have gone to prison and to death with Paul and the long list of martyrs that stretches through the centuries. The life of the prophet is much the same in every age. The servant is not above his Master. So far, at least, the redemption of the world has been achieved through self-sacrificing and suffering.

"The real questions which confront the Christian minister of to-day are: (1) The question of his own call to the ministry; (2) the question of his faith in God's redemptive processes, and (3) the question of his courage to endure those processes as he finds them expressed in modern life.

"Our age is in danger of making redemptive suffering a theory which found sufficient expression 2,000 years ago in Jesus Christ. Paul teaches that Christians—and it must be preëminently true of Christian ministers—are to fill up the measure of Christ's suffering. The redemptive suffering that starts people on the way to Christ is suffering that comes upon us to-day, and is brought upon us by present conditions, and which we endure for Christ's sake.

"Do not think that I am unsympathetic with your discouragement, old friend, but you know that you are only one of many ministers at this time who are leaving the ministry for secular work, though all may not be as frank as you in stating the reasons. I am only expressing to you what has occurred to me many times before, viz., the conviction that a more heroic note needs to be struck for the Christian ministry to-day, a note which rings true to the spirit of the prophets, the Christ, and the apostles."

5. *Renunciation*

"But we have renounced the hidden things of shame, not walking in craftiness, nor handling the word of God deceitfully."[1] This is a very remarkable passage and strikes deep into the minister's heart and life. Paul evidently has before him the bitter Judaizers at Corinth who had been full of schemes and plots against Paul and the work of Christ. Paul had bidden "the hidden things" of shame be gone. He had declined[2] every suggestion and impulse that would not bear the light. "The hidden things of shame"[3] are all those things which one's sense of honour does not allow to come to the light. He does not specify further. If you lift a rock in the spring-time, the bugs flee from the light. The preacher's heart is not to be the receptacle of private vengeance, ecclesiastical plots, impure thoughts of any kind. "Renounce the devil and all his works"[4] is a good interpretation of Paul's idea. One who looks constantly into the face of Christ will not wish to revel in the hidden things of shame. A preacher can overdo the "slumming" business and make it a satisfaction of morbid curiosity instead of real desire to help the erring. Paul mentions two particulars of the hidden things of shame. One is "walking in craftiness." The word for craftiness[5] means being willing to resort to any practice to carry one's point. The end does not justify the means

[1] 2 Cor. iv. 2.
[2] Renounced.
[3] Cf. 1 Cor. iv. 5, the hidden things of darkness.
[4] The Prayer-Book.
[5] Cf. 2 Cor. xi. 3.

with Paul nor with Christ. The minister does his best work in the open. He opens his own heart to God and to the people. That is his strength. He is stronger without the veil. The other particular is "handling the word of God deceitfully."[1] Both of these things the Judaizers did. They had made a misuse and a misapplication of the Word of God. The devil could quote Scripture. He is never happier than when he can get preachers to do his work.[2] "And no marvel; for even Satan fashioneth himself into an angel of light." The wreckers who wave false lights on the coast to lure unsuspecting ships to ruin are no worse than men who wilfully twist the Word of God to their own selfish schemes and purposes. Paul had spoken of this matter once before.[3] The Word of God calls for honesty of interpretation and exposition. Intellectual honesty is a first essential in a true preacher. The prophet of Christ is no mere juggler of words. He is dealing with the most serious and sacred things in life and must speak with frankness of mind and heart. "Observe St. Paul's argument: We do not tamper with the Word of God. It is not concealed or darkened by us; for our very work is to spread light, to throw sunshine on every side, and in every way fearlessly to declare the truth, to dread no consequences; for no real minister

[1] Cf. 1 Pet. iii. 10. [2] 2 Cor. xi. 15. [3] 2 Cor. ii. 17.

of Christ can be afraid of illumination."[1] The man who looks in the face of Christ looks up and not down. He looks all men in the eye.

6. *Manifestation of the Truth*

"But by the manifestation of the truth commending ourselves to every man's conscience in the sight of God."[2] This is Paul's policy as a minister of Christ, perfect candour, in contrast to the conduct of the Judaizers. They had accused him of all sorts of tricks, none of which were true. This was his letter of commendation,[3] viz., the full truth. He commended himself by telling the truth. The word for truth[4] means unconcealed. The lid is removed that all may see. The word "manifestation"[5] goes well with truth. "We spake all things to you in truth."[6] The preacher's province is that of truth. He has no call to any other realm. Pilate was ignorant of the kingdom of truth of which Jesus is King and did not see that such an abstract ideality interfered at all with the rule of Cæsar. But the interpreter of Jesus, who is the truth, while hospitable to all truth both speculative and concrete, is not directly concerned with the pursuit of absolute theoretical truth. Scien-

[1] F. W. Robertson, "Life and Letters," etc., p. 628.
[2] 2 Cor. iv. 2.
[3] Cf. 2 Cor. iii. 1.
[4] Cf. 2 Cor. xi. 10, the truth of Christ.
[5] Cf. 1 Cor. xii. 7.
[6] 2 Cor. vii. 14.

tific research *per se* and as an end in itself is not the function of the preacher. Certainly philosophy as usually taught does not cross the path of the preacher. The minister is a pragmatist in fact, whatever he is in theory. The truth which the preacher is to manifest is the realm of spiritual reality and practical ethics, not speculative ontology and cosmology. The preacher grips the conscience of men. He misses the mark when he appeals merely to intellectual curiosity, æsthetic interest, or the pleasures of the imagination or emotions. The conscience and the will must be confronted[1] with Christ. "The appeal to conscience can never be omitted with safety, and any presentation of Christianity which is neglectful of the verdict of conscience on the doctrines taught is at once un-apostolic and un-Christlike."[2] It is only by placing his plea on this highest plane that the minister has authority. Clothed with truth he has the right to storm the citadel of every man's heart. It is this that makes the real preacher the master of men. Men are so busy with things that they neglect themselves—their best selves—and God. The truth comes as a rude shock. "It is the evil heart which hides the truth. Light shines on all—that is, all who are in a natural human state, all who can feel, all who have not deadened the spiritual

[1] *Pros.*

[2] Bernard, *in loco.*

sense. . . . The evidence of the sun is its light and not the shadow on the dial. So Christ is divine to those who are of the truth."[1] If one sees Christ clearly, he has redemptive truth. It is well also if he can add speculative truth about the world, but that is distinctly secondary. The old war between philosophy and religion is disappearing. Professor James, of Harvard, has won for religion the right of fair treatment from philosophy as a fact in itself worthy of study. It is by no means certain that philosophy will ever understand religion.[2] We need not seek to define more closely Paul's use of "truth" and "conscience." He is no slave of words nor does he set forth a developed and consistent formula of psychological terms. He makes his appeal to the moral judgment of man and does it in the fullness of truth.[3]

7. *A Veiled Gospel*

"And even if our gospel is veiled, it is veiled in them that perish: in whom the God of this world hath blinded the minds of the unbelieving, that the light of the Gospel of the glory of Christ, who is the image of God, should not dawn upon them."[4] Paul

[1] F. W. Robertson, "Life and Letters," etc., p. 628.
[2] "Religion and Philosophy," by T. M. Watt, in "Mansfield College Essays," p. 334.
[3] Cf. "Hebrew Psychology in Relation to Pauline Anthropology," by H. W. Robinson, in "Mansfield College Essays," p. 267 ff.
[4] 2 Cor. iv. 3 f.

had manifested the truth, had declared his Gospel of the glory of Christ. There was no excuse for those who heard if they did not understand. There is no veil over the face of Christ. There is no veil over the face of Paul and the other ministers of the New Covenant. There is no veil over the Gospel as preached by Paul. But it is a sad fact that there is a veil over the hearts of many who hear as there was a veil over the hearts of the Jews who read Moses and could not see the Messiah in Jesus.[1] It is a sad situation with which Paul is confronted. In Romans ix.–xi. he will soon be explaining how God is still true to His Word though the great mass of the Jews have rejected the Gospel of Christ. The spiritual Israel he interprets as the real Israel of promise and this Israel included both Gentiles and Jews. The children of faith are the heirs of the promise. Every minister of the Gospel meets a like situation in his work. "The Gospel remains a secret, an impotent ineffective secret, to many who hear it again and again. Paul faces the difficulty without flinching, though the answer is appalling."[2] It is sometimes true, beyond doubt, that the minister has not done his full duty. He has not understood the problem

[1] The condition in 2 Cor. iv. 3 is of the first class (determined as fulfilled) and assumes the statement as a fact. Cf. Robertson, "Short Grammar of the Greek New Testament," p. 161.

[2] Denney, 2 Corinthians, p. 148.

in this particular field or he has not delivered the message with sufficient clearness, ability or earnestness. Every preacher has his moments of sorrow over such shortcomings. But that is not the point made here by Paul. He does not claim perfection for himself. What he says is that many have wilfully shut their eyes to the light in the face of Jesus. They have let "the god of this world" blind their minds so that they cannot understand. He is using language like that of the rabbis who called "Sammael" the "second god." He was the evil spirit who was considered the special foe of Israel.[1] Jesus called Satan "the prince of this world."[2] Paul alluded to some who made a god of their belly.[3] This warning is peculiarly pertinent just now when mammon has such a hold on the hearts of men as is seen in the mad race for money at the cost of principle, virtue of men and women, law and order, love of man and God. The Pharisees were lovers of money.[4] Paul found money to be a root of all kinds of evil.[5] But there is much more than money which is here involved. The spirit of worldliness opposes religion, resents the effort to check desires of the flesh, opposes real Christianity though willing to compromise with the forms of public worship if no effort

[1] Wetstein, *in loco.* Cf. Bernard, *in loco.*
[2] John xii. 31.
[3] Phil. iii. 19.
[4] Luke xvi. 14.
[5] 1 Tim. vi. 10.

is made to make people really spiritual and good, is rightly called by Paul "the god of this age." The time-spirit (*Zeitgeist*) has amazing success in putting out the eyes of the modern Samsons and making them grind the treadmill of material things to the neglect and death of the spiritual aspirations and life. Hear Denney:[1] "What sleepy conscience, what moral mediocrity, itself purblind, only dimly conscious of the height of the Christian calling, and vexed by no aspirations towards it, has any right to say that it is too much to call Satan 'the god of this world'?" As already explained, it is possible that "in them that perish: in whom" may be taken as "by the perishing things by which."[2] At any rate it is by flaunting before the eyes of the unbelieving the perishing toys of earth that the god of this world blinds the hearts of men to the glory of Christ and the worth of the spiritual life. "Men who find their all in the world—how can they, fevered by its business, excited by its pleasures, petrified by its maxims, see God in His purity, or comprehend the calm radiance of eternity?"[3] Jesus[4] and Paul[5] both saw in the hardness of men's hearts the fulfillment of Isaiah's prophecy.

[1] 2 Corinthians, p. 156.
[2] The gender may be neuter in the Greek.
[3] F. W. Robertson, "Life and Letters," etc., p. 629.
[4] John xii. 37-41.
[5] Acts xxviii. 25-28.

8. *From Glory to Glory*

The Apostle Paul was a firm believer in progress. By this phrase[1] he aptly sets forth the spiritual development of all those who keep in constant touch with the glory of Christ. The joy of his life was the hope of making more progress. He had a holy discontent with what he had already done and an eager impetuosity to push on "towards the goal unto the prize of the high calling of God in Christ Jesus."[2] The more Paul saw of Jesus the more dissatisfied he became with himself. The progress that Paul is here thinking of is not increased reputation, power, influence. Those are mere accidents, though I am glad to quote this sentence from Dr. J. Wilbur Chapman: "Never was there such a day as this for the preacher." Paul is contemplating a richer personality, one more like Jesus, one more completely surrendered to the Spirit, one that more effectively reflects the glory of God to men. It is in sooth a good thing when a minister's development is manifest to all.[3] That is a ground of rejoicing. The saints of God delight in a minister who knows how to handle the Word of God rightly, who is meet for the Master's use, prepared unto every good work.[4] But Paul does not mean for the preacher himself to be marking notches in his

[1] 2 Cor. iii. 18. [2] Phil. iii. 14. [3] 1 Tim. iv. 15.
[4] 2 Tim. ii. 15, 21.

progress. The man who has made most spiritual development may be least conscious of it. Certainly there can be no posing for effect nor attitudinizing on the part of the man who has entered most into the heart of Jesus, who has gazed longest at the glory of Christ, who has been most completely transfigured into the likeness of Christ. That man will see more clearly the sins in his heart in the clear white light of the Cross. There are higher heights of glory ahead and the Face of Christ beckons on. Some day "we shall be like Him; for we shall see Him even as He is."[1]

[1] I John iii. 2.

V

THIS TREASURE IN EARTHEN VESSELS —THE HUMAN LIMITATIONS

(2 Cor. iv. 7–15)

> "But we have this treasure in earthen vessels, that the exceeding greatness of the power may be of God, and not from ourselves."
>
> —*2 Cor. iv. 7.*

V

THIS TREASURE IN EARTHEN VESSELS—THE HUMAN LIMITATIONS

1. *The Weaknesses of Preachers*

IT is not clear whether the sudden contrast between the precious "light of the knowledge of the glory of God in the face of Jesus Christ" and the feeble and imperfect medium through which this "Gospel of the glory of Christ" is conveyed to men is suggested to Paul by the inherent facts in the case or also by taunts of his enemies about his own personal weaknesses.[1] Later in the Epistle Paul does reveal knowledge of the sneers made against him and his work in Corinth. "For his letters, they say, are weighty and strong; but his bodily presence is weak, and his speech is of no account."[2] This was a personal stab at the defects of his bodily presence, otherwise unknown to us, for the traditions about his being a hunchback and having weak eyes have no support in Paul's Epistles unless weak eyes are suggested by Galatians iv. 15: "Ye would have plucked out your eyes and given them to me." But he did once, if not always, have "a temptation to

[1] See Meyer, *in loco*, and Bachmann, *in loco*. [2] 2 Cor. x. 10.

you in my flesh "[1] which the Galatians had not despised. In spite of this they had received him "as an angel of God, even as Christ Jesus" would have been welcomed. Evidently Paul was conscious of bodily imperfections and limitations. He had no disposition to pose as a martyr because of his defects. He mentions his "weakness"[2] because his enemies had flung it in his face, so to speak. He had his "thorn in the flesh," whatever it was (a blessed ignorance to all ministers who have thus a delicate bond of union with Paul), and had learned how to bear his burden, even to "take pleasure in weaknesses, in injuries, in necessities, in persecutions, in distresses, for Christ's sake; for when I am weak, then am I strong."[3] To his prayer for the removal of the thorn, he had this answer: "My grace is sufficient for thee: for My power is made perfect in weakness." That hard lesson Paul, like the rest of us, had to learn by long experience. Some of the enemies of Paul criticized his preaching. "His speech is of no account." This probably means that he will be afraid to say in speech what he writes in letters rather than depreciation of his style of utterance. Paul made no claim to great oratory[4] and knew that he did not please

[1] Gal. iv. 14. [2] 2 Cor. xi. 30. [3] 2 Cor. xii. 10.
[4] 1 Cor. ii. 2.

all men. "I was with you in weakness, and in fear, and in much trembling. And my speech and my preaching were not in persuasive words of wisdom."[1] It was a constant wonder[2] to Paul that Jesus could have found any good in him as a minister of the Gospel, one who had been "a blasphemer, and a persecutor, and injurious." He still felt himself to be the chief of sinners. There may have been an undertone of acknowledgment of the taunts of his enemies in this comparison. The preacher is surely placed in an embarrassing position when he becomes the target of personal criticism from people who are themselves anything but perfect. He is not able to stand up and speak for himself, if he has the spirit of humility and knows how frail after all he is. There is exquisite suffering in many a minister's heart as a result of cutting, heartless criticisms of his person, his speech, and his life. One must not be oversensitive, least of all pretend to be perfect or above criticism. The note that Paul strikes here is the chord of sympathy. "There is less of polemical argument, and more of the natural outpouring of his own feelings in this section, than in most other parts of the Epistle."[3] "We have this treasure in earthen vessels."[4] It is, beyond all doubt, a matter of surprise

[1] 1 Cor. ii. 3. [2] 1 Tim. i. 12 ff. [3] Stanley, *in loco*. [4] Cf. 2 Tim. ii. 20.

that God should entrust this matchless treasure to feeble instruments whom the axe and the lion can destroy.[1] "The disproportion between his [man's] own nature and powers, and the high calling to which he has been called, flashes across his mind."[2] The vessel of clay[3] is very fragile and is easily broken and destroyed. Yet to-day the *ostraka*, broken pieces of pottery picked up in the sands of Egypt, are bearing eloquent testimony to the life of the people in Paul's own time.[4] The Persian kings kept their gold and silver in earthenware jars.[5] There is a rabbinical story of Rabbi Joshua who was taunted by the emperor's daughter on his mean appearance. He pointed to the earthen jars which contained her father's wines. She then placed the wine in silver vessels when it turned sour, whereon the rabbi ventured to remind her that the humblest vessels sometimes contained the highest wisdom.[6] The use of "earthen vessel" as a figure for man's littleness as compared with God's greatness is frequent.[7] He is like the potter's clay. There are, to be sure, differences in men.[8] They do not all have precisely the same frailties and limitations, but they all have them.

[1] F. W. Robertson, "Life and Letters," etc., p. 629.
[2] Denney, *in loco*.
[3] *Ostrakinos*.
[4] Cf. Deissmann, "Light from the Ancient East."
[5] Herodotus, Vol. III, p. 96.
[6] Cf. Stanley, *in loco*, and Wetstein.
[7] Cf. Job x. 9; Isa. xxx. 14; Jer. xix. 11; 2 Esdras iv. 11; Rom. ix. 20 ff.; 2 Tim. ii. 20.
[8] 2 Tim. ii. 20.

The church that is looking for perfection at a thousand dollars a year or at ten thousand will look in vain. It is a fearful mistake to expect or demand an impossible standard in the preacher. There can only result dissatisfaction. Ministers are men and so long as other men are not perfect, there is no hope of perfection in the ministry. If God could not use poor instruments and feeble voices, He would make no music. Socrates disdained the title of teacher and called himself a fellow-inquirer.[1] There is, of course, small consolation in noting the defects of other men, but in this view it is necessary to get the true perspective. Abraham was guilty of duplicity, and yet he became the man of faith and the friend of God. Moses had his halting speech and quick temper, yet he was the man chosen to make a nation and to commune with God. David was guilty of adultery and murder, but he repented and became a man after God's own heart and the sweet singer of Israel for all time. Elijah ran from Jezebel and sat under the juniper tree, but he had stood on Carmel and defied Ahab and all the prophets of Baal and he heard the still small voice of God at Horeb. Isaiah, in the presence of the heavenly vision of God's holiness, said:[2] "Woe is me! for I am undone; because

[1] Adam, "Religious Teachers of Greece," p. 339.

[2] Isa. vi. 5. Cf. Stalker, "The Preacher and His Models," pp. 46 ff.

I am a man of unclean lips, and I dwell in the midst of a people of unclean lips; for mine eyes have seen the King Jehovah of Hosts." Nevertheless, he ventured to say, after one of the seraphim touched his lips with a coal from the altar and cleansed his lips: "Here am I; send me." And Peter, who, though the leader and spokesman of the Twelve Apostles, had denied his Lord with oaths and curses, was restored by the compassion of Jesus and was able to speak under the power of the Holy Spirit with tremendous effect on the Day of Pentecost. It is needless to go on. There was John the Apostle, who expected to be praised by Jesus for refusing to allow a man not of their company to cast out demons in the name of Jesus, who with James wanted to call down fire from heaven to burn up a Samaritan village, who with James, also, wanted the chief places in the kingdom of Jesus—John became the Beloved Disciple, the apostle of love, the eagle who soared to great heights, who pierced the deepest into the mystery of Christ the Son of God.

2. *The Exceeding Greatness of the Power of God*

There is no doubt of the fact of the human limitations of ministers of Christ. Some even make complete shipwreck like Judas whom the devil captured completely. Satan tempted all the other apostles, as he did Christ Himself. The servant is not above his Lord. Every preacher is from the very nature of the case a target of the devil. Satan wanted to sift all the apostles like wheat and Jesus made special prayer for Peter.[1] People sometimes forget that preachers are subject to temptation and innocently throw temptations across their path. To speak plainly, preachers may fall victims to silly women, to love of money, and to love of praise. "But thou, O man of God, flee these things."[2] The very fact that God can do so much with such frail men as ministers of necessity are is proof of the greatness of God's power. Indeed, Paul boldly interprets this to be God's purpose.[3] This was the reason God had refused to remove the thorn in the flesh of Paul. He was in danger of being exalted overmuch by reason of the visions given him. But now he had this perpetual reminder of his human weakness, "that the power of Christ may rest upon me."[4] The word[5] of Paul means "shooting beyond the mark," beyond all measurement. There is no limit to the power of God. There is thus no limit to the work of the preacher, though an earthen vessel. People are often

[1] Luke xxii. 31 f.

[2] 1 Tim. vi. 11. The false prophets in the Old Testament present a terrible picture. "The prophets prophesy falsely, and my people love to have it so," Jeremiah laments. Cf. especially Jer. xxiii. 9–40; Ezek. xiii. See Stalker, "The Preacher and His Models," Lecture V.

[3] 2 Cor. iv. 7. [4] 2 Cor. xii. 5, 7 ff. [5] Cf. iv. 17.

astonished at the results of a given ministry. The preaching is not eloquent, is not learned, is not always attractive. Men have been puzzled to analyze the power of D. L. Moody. God is the only explanation. Moody had really great powers, but gave himself wholly to God and God filled him with His own power. Paul had already explained to the Corinthians that God worked thus, "that your faith should not stand in the wisdom of men, but in the power of God."[1] The increase came from God. Preachers do differ, but each receives his gift from God and a *gift* is not an occasion for pride or selfish bickering, but of humble gratitude. "For who makest thee to differ? and what hast thou that thou didst not receive?"[2] Spurgeon, Maclaren, Newman, Liddon, Parker, Beecher, Brooks, Broadus, Moody,—each had his own gift from God. These were the mighty in the generation just gone, "not many wise after the flesh, not many mighty, not many noble." "God chose the foolish things of the world, that He might put to shame them that are wise; and God chose the weak things of the world, that He might put to shame the things that are strong; and the base things of the world, and the

[1] 1 Cor. ii. 5.

[2] 1 Cor. iv. 7. I shall never forget a masterly address delivered to the students of the Southern Baptist Theological Seminary many years ago by Archibald G. Brown from this text.

things that are despised, did God choose, yea and the things that are not, that He might bring to naught the things that are: that no flesh should glory before God."[1] This is the perennial lesson of the preacher, that of God's power. Look at the stripling in all his awkward timidity, but full of a deep earnestness to answer the call of God for service. See him years afterwards as he moves the multitude to repentance. That is the power of God, the exceeding greatness of His power. "No one who saw this, and looked at a preacher like Paul, could dream that the explanation lay in *him*. Not in an ugly little Jew, without presence, without eloquence, without the means to bribe or to compel, could the source of such courage, the cause of such transformations, be found; it must be sought, not in him, but in God."[2] Hear Denney[3] again: "One would sometimes think, from the tone of current literature, that no person with gifts above contempt is any longer identified with the Gospel. Clever men, we are told, do not become preachers now, still less do they go to church. . . . There always have been men in the world so clever that God could make no use of them; they could never do His work, because they were so lost in admiration of their own. But God's work never depended on

[1] 1 Cor. i. 26–29. [2] Denney, *in loco*. [3] P. 160.

them, and it does not depend on them now." That is well said and to the point. But it needs to be added that those "clever" men do not always know greatness of intellect, not to say character, when they see it. A tenth-rate novel with its cheap jibes at the ministry may pass as "literature" with the unthinking and it will be forgotten to-morrow. It is easy to set up a man of straw and caricature the preacher. Manhood is the first essential in the minister. "Our first minister was a man, but he was not a minister; our second was a minister, but he was not a man; and the one we have at present is neither a man nor a minister."[1] The preacher must have "the blood-streak of experience."[2] This Paul had. He had sympathy, heart, and was the "Man of Tears."[3] But he was also a man of transcendent intellectual gifts. It is taking nothing from the power of God to note that this chosen vessel to bear the Gospel to the Gentiles was just the most gifted man of his time in all the real elements of human greatness. "Every now and then, his thought bursts up through the argument like a flaming geyser and falls in showers of sparks," and, like Shakespeare, he will "pause and, spreading his wings, go soaring and

[1] Stalker, "The Preacher and His Models," p. 165. The experience of a Scotch Highlander. "People do not now respect the cloth, unless they find a man inside it."

[2] *Ibid.*, p. 166. [3] Adolph Monod, "The Tears of Paul."

singing like a lark sheer up into the blue."[1] It does not lie in the mouth of any modern man to ridicule the intellectual prowess of Paul. The ministry of Christ makes its appeal to the men of the noblest gifts, but God is not dependent on any set of men. The student life of our time will miss the supreme opportunity for usefulness if it passes by the claims of the ministry of Christ. But it must not be forgotten that Jesus chose His apostles from the unschooled fishermen and artisans of Galilee save Judas the Judean. He passed by the rabbinical theological seminaries where religious impulse had died and thought had crystallized. He will pass by the schools to-day if the teachers and students close their minds and hearts to Him. Jesus seeks the open mind and the warm heart. He knocks at the door of the heart of every university and seminary man in the world. The answer is more important to the student than it is to Christ. Jesus will go to the highways and find others to heed His call, but the student will not find another Christ to serve. At best it is only an earthen vessel that any one can offer, wholly unworthy of the priceless jewel which Jesus offers to place therein. Who can ask for a higher service than to tell of the Light in the Face of Jesus Christ?

[1] Stalker, "The Preacher and His Models," p. 158.

3. *The Guiding Hand*

The secret of success in the ministry is very simple. It is real connection with God, vital union with Christ. This is just the most difficult thing to maintain in fullness of life. The strains of life pull us away. Dust gathers about our heads and in our eyes. Clouds gather and the sun does not shine upon us. God seems to slip away from us and we are left with our weakness and the criticism of the people. It is not human weakness that is a source of strength. It is only when the power of God charges the empty vessel that it becomes a dynamo. Paul changes the figure from that of an earthen vessel to a soldier, with an anacoluthon so common in this Epistle: "Pressed on every side, yet not straitened."[1] He was "hard pressed, but not driven into straits."[2] He was not yet hemmed in, not put into a corner. He could still go on with his work.[3] God had always come to his rescue. The old negro's philosophy comes in here: "It mout be wuss." Paul carries on the contrast between human weakness and God's power: "perplexed, yet not unto despair."[4] He had lost his way,[5] he was bewildered like a man going in a circle, he was "put to it, yet

[1] 2 Cor. iv. 8; cf. Rom. ii. 9; viii. 35.
[2] Meyer, *in loco.*
[3] Cf. 2 Cor. xii. 10.
[4] 2 Cor. iv. 8.
[5] Cf. Gal. iv. 20.

not utterly put out."[1] How these phrases parallel the experience of every minister of Jesus. We come to our wit's end and find God there. Man's extremity is God's opportunity. We are "pursued, yet not forsaken."[2] He was hunted like a wild animal, yet not abandoned to the pursuing foe. How often, when persecuted, Paul had to flee for his life! We were "pursued in our flight, but not left behind as a prey to our pursuers."[3] Once more: "smitten down, yet not destroyed."[4] The image may be of one smitten down with a dart or arrow or of one overtaken in flight and thrown to the ground. He had himself been stoned and left for dead. But he did not perish, not yet. When trouble has done its worst, he has been able to rise from the ground and go on proclaiming Christ. The hand of God in his life Paul here joyfully acknowledges. This is the sustaining power in life. This he has always had.

4. *The Lesson of Suffering*

This is the climax of the series of contrasts. Paul is not merely resigned to suffering and persecution. Others, not Christians, have come to that state with more or less success. Paul has come to rejoice in his sufferings as filling up that which is lacking of

[1] Denney, *in loco.*
[2] Cf. Gal. i. 13.
[3] Stanley, *in loco.*
[4] *Kataballo.*

the afflictions of Christ.[1] He is dying daily.[2] He is killed all the day long.[3] This continual exposure to the peril of death is like the experience of Jesus. So then Paul "is always bearing about in the body the dying of Jesus."[4] He has no complaint to make on this score. It is part of the business of the follower of Jesus, the soldier of the Cross: "For we who live are always delivered unto death for Jesus' sake."[5] The soldier does not flinch when the bullets whizz by his head nor when they strike his heart. Besides, Paul knows that "the sufferings which come upon him daily in his work for Jesus are gradually killing him; the pains, the perils, the spiritual pressure, the excitement of danger and the excitement of deliverance, are wearing out his strength, and soon he must die."[6] He, like Jesus, was facing a certain death, hastened by the very work in which he was engaged. But his hand was to the plough and he would not turn back. "It is as if he had said, 'we are living corpses. We bear with us wherever we go the burden of the dead body.'"[7] But there is a purpose in it all. Thus it is that the life of Christ is reproduced in us, "that the life also of Jesus may be manifested in our body."[8] Jesus had said that the man who lost his life would

[1] Col. i. 24. [2] 1 Cor. xv. 31. [3] Rom. viii. 36.
[4] 2 Cor. iv. 10. [5] 2 Cor. iv. 11.
[6] Denney, *in loco.* [7] Stanley, *in loco.* [8] 2 Cor. iv. 10.

find it.[1] "Christ, then, is the mystic symbol of Christian life; His death and resurrection are repeated in His people. . . . Pain was sacred, since Christ had also suffered. Life became grand when viewed as a repetition of the life of Christ."[2] Besides, "death worketh in us, but life in you."[3] There is divine energy [4] in death itself and the slow dying before Paul was working out for the good of the saints who were benefited by his ministry. Paul does not look on suffering as an accident, but as a matter of divine appointment that thus the fullness of the life of Christ may be presented to men.[5] Calvin [6] calls this saying of Paul in verse twelve ironical. That is true of 1 Corinthians iv. 8, but hardly here. It is part of the equipment of every preacher that he enter the valley of the shadow of death. Only thus is he qualified to bind up broken hearts, to give a sympathetic heart to those who need that more than mere words. The Messiah was to be a man of sorrows and acquainted with grief. Brilliant as was Paul's intellect, it is probable that his heart was greater than his head.[7] "Who is weak and I am not weak? Who is caused to stumble and I burn not?"[8]

[1] Matt. x. 39.
[2] F. W. Robertson, "Life and Letters," etc., p. 631.
[3] 2 Cor. iv. 12. [4] *Energeital.* [5] Denney, *in loco.*
[6] *In loco. Ironice dictum.*
[7] Stalker, "The Preacher and His Models," p. 159.
[8] 2 Cor. xi. 29.

"Our mouth is open unto you, O Corinthians, our heart is enlarged. . . . Open your hearts to us."[1]

5. *The Power of Conviction*

"I believed, and therefore did I speak; we also believe, and therefore also we speak."[2] Paul has applied the words of the Psalmist[3] to his own case. The spirit of faith is essential to the preacher. Distrust of God cuts the nerve of faith and renders the preacher powerless. It is just this trust in Christ which is the channel through which flows the power of God into the earthen vessel. Without trust there is no conviction. No positive note is struck by the minister who does not love and trust Christ. It is useless for him to chatter away about the beauty of duty and the æsthetics of social service when the fire of love for Christ does not burn in his own heart. "We also believe, and therefore we also speak."[4] If one does not believe, let him at least be silent and not attempt to expound his doubts. People care nothing for them and are not profited by them. When the doubter comes back to Christ, then he has a message for men.[5] "The minister of Christ speaks in faith; that is, in a firm conviction of divine power arising from the Resurrection—faith in the deliver-

[1] 2 Cor. vii. 2, 11.
[2] 2 Cor. iv. 13.
[3] Psa. cxvi. 10, but LXX cxv. i.
[4] 2 Cor. iv. 13.
[5] Cf. George Romanes, "Thoughts on Religion."

ing or redeeming power of God. Observe the difference between this and theological knowledge. It is not a minister's wisdom, but his *conviction*, which imparts itself to others. Nothing gives life but life. Real flame alone kindles other flame."[1] Men with that *will* speak and will be heard also. "For we cannot but speak the things which we saw and heard."[2] So Paul felt: "For woe is unto me, if I preach not the Gospel."[3] The necessity was laid upon him which drove him forward in the service of Christ. A man with profound conviction will not so much be hunting for something to say as be eager for an opportunity to say what fills his mind and heart. Paul has a contempt for mere intellectualism divorced from experience.[4] The preacher should be constantly engaged in "Great Reading," the reading of great books, and not be frightened by the bugbear of simplicity into making his sermons thin and watery.[5] But no amount of reading nor intellectual brilliance will take the place of thorough conviction and sincerity.

6. *Thanksgiving*

"For all things are for your sakes, that the grace, being multiplied through the many, may cause the

[1] F. W. Robertson, "Life and Letters," p. 629.
[2] Acts iv. 20.
[3] I Cor. ix. 16
[4] Stalker, "The Preacher and His Models," p. 253.
[5] *Ibid.*, pp. 252 f.

thanksgiving to abound unto the glory of God."[1] Paul expects that God will present[2] him and his converts together at the court of heaven before Christ Jesus. That will be a joyful scene. Paul will be grateful for what God has wrought through him in them. They will thank God for Paul. It is possible to be thankful for the ministry with all these shortcomings.[3] Certainly the grace of God merits thanksgiving. That grace is in most cases conveyed in these earthen vessels. Suppose we had no preachers of the Gospel. Thought along that line will surely afford abundant ground for thankfulness for the ministers, taking them as they are. It might be far worse. Let us then praise God for His grace and for His ministers of grace. We must make our thanksgiving articulate, not taciturn,[4] that it may "abound unto the glory of God," may overflow[5] and bless others. The minister bathes his heart and life in the light of the knowledge of the glory of God in the face of Jesus Christ. As he reflects that glory upon others, he adds to the praise of the glory of God among men. "A minister is no true minister who does not see wonder in the child in the cradle and in the peasant in the field."[6] Yes, and who does not win the love of peasant and child.

[1] 2 Cor. iv. 15.
[2] *Parastēsei.*
[3] Cf. 1 Cor. iii. 22; Phil. i. 19.
[4] Denney, *in loco.*
[5] *Perisseuo.*
[6] Stalker, "The Preacher and His Models," p. 283.

VI

THE WEIGHT OF GLORY—THE INVISIBLE CONSOLATION

(*2 Cor. iv. 16–v. 8*)

"While we look not at the things which are seen, but at the things which are not seen."

—*2 Cor. iv. 18.*

VI

THE WEIGHT OF GLORY—THE INVISIBLE CONSOLATION

"WE faint not," Paul repeats from verse one. He faces all the facts of life and sees no ground for despair. Paul is not yet an old man, though probably the marks of care and toil and exposure were upon his face. He was discouraged before Titus came, but that was not his normal mood. He caught a fresh glimpse of the Face of Christ and his soul has been singing like the wood robin. He has taken stock of his ministry in comparison with that of the Old Covenant. He has looked afresh at his own shortcomings. He has looked death in the face, but he is not dismayed. Once more Paul is brought face to face with the eternal verities of life. He does not shrink from the look and all that it means. He ventures to interpret the most sacred realities of the preacher's heart. What weighs most in the scales of life, in the minister's life?

1. *The Growth of the Inward Man*

"Though our outward man is decaying, yet our inward man is renewed day by day."[1] There is no

[1] 2 Cor. iv. 16.

rebellion in Paul's heart as he faces old age and death. One of the most beautiful spectacles in all the world is that of an old minister with a young heart, who has learned how to grow old gracefully and be a benediction to all about him. Paul is constantly surrounded by a band of young preachers who fill his heart with joy as he sees them enter the thick of the fight with him. These young ministers are "willing to follow him through fire and water."[1] There is no "dead-line" for Paul. The older a minister becomes the richer he is in spiritual knowledge and power. Alexander Maclaren at eighty years of age was a greater personality than at fifty.[2] A man's intellectual and spiritual decay comes when he ceases to study, to work, to exercise, to grow. It is a minister's duty not to be prodigal of his physical strength, to use his physical force with wisdom and power for God, but a minister can be too particular with himself for any use in the world. It is better to wear out than to rust out, though there is no special call for one to hurry up the process of decay. But "Paul could not mistake, and did not hide from himself, the effect which his apostolic work had upon him. He saw it was killing him. He was old long before his time. He was a sorely broken

[1] Stalker, "The Preacher and His Models," p. 161.
[2] Some churches are guilty of a crime in closing the door of usefulness in the face of the greatest men because old.

man at an age when many are in the fullness of their strength. The earthen vessel was visibly crumbling."[1] The exposures and hardships thrust upon Paul by his enemies had left their mark[2] in many ways. The end of this gradual dissolution is bound to be death sooner or later.[3] Decay[4] has become visible in "the outward man."[5] Paul has not spoken of "the outward man" elsewhere, though he uses "the old man"[6] in the sense of the lower fleshly nature. Here he means the material nature, the physical abode of the spirit, the body. The minister has his physical trials as have others. The missionaries in all ages give a vivid picture of Paul's case, as, for instance, Adoniram Judson at Oung-Pen-La. But the consolation is real and glorious. Paul is "sustained by a glorious hope."[7] The inward man is renewed day by day.[8] "The more the marble wastes, the more the statue grows."[9] It is true of all men that the outward man decays. "Time tires the stoutest runner, crumbles the compactest wall."[10] But it is not, alas, true of all that there is a daily refreshment of "the inner man." This expression he uses twice elsewhere.[11] It is a

[1] Denney, *in loco*. [2] Gal. vi. 17. [3] Stanley, *in loco*.
[4] *Diaphtheiretai*.
[5] The condition here assumes the reality of the decay.
[6] Cf. Eph. iv. 22; Col. iii. 9. [7] Bernard, *in loco*. [8] 2 Cor. iv. 16.
[9] Line attributed to Michael Angelo. Cf. Stanley, *in loco*.
[10] Denney, *in loco*. [11] Rom. vii. 2; Eph. iii. 16.

most expressive figure for the spiritual and moral nature. He uses "the new man"[1] in contrast with "the old man" as a description of the new life in Christ after regeneration. One who is in Christ is a new creature (creation).[2] One puts off the old man and puts on the new man like a new garment.[3] He does not here mean the new birth by "renewed" as he does by another word in Ephesians iv. 23,[4] nor is he exactly contemplating the progressive restoration of the image of God by the work of sanctification as in Colossians iii. 10.[5] Here Paul is thinking of "the daily supply of spiritual power for apostolic service."[6] He is as one whose youth is renewed like the eagle. Each morning brings fresh supply of grace like manna from heaven. He is ready for the new day by reason of the new and never-failing store of spiritual energy which is communicated to him. "When I am weak, then am I strong"[7] with a strength not his own. With Paul it is the triumph of the moral and spiritual forces over the material decay. He is strengthened with might by the Spirit in the inner man.[8] The minister who thus lives in vital contact with God is never old. He can laugh at disease, decay, and death. "The Lord stood by

[1] Cf. Col. iii. 10.
[2] Cf. 2 Cor. iii. 17.
[3] Eph. iv. 24; Col. iii. 10.
[4] Cf. also Tit. iii. 5.
[5] Cf. Rom. xii. 2.
[6] Denney, *in loco*.
[7] 2 Cor. xii. 10.
[8] Eph. iii. 16.

me, and strengthened me,"[1] Paul will say at the end as he looks death squarely in the face. Yea, says Paul, "I can do all things in Him that strengtheneth me."[2] This is the mighty preacher, he who puts the chief accent on the development of spiritual muscle and fibre for the work of Christ.

2. *The Work of Affliction*

"For our light affliction, which is for the moment, worketh for us more and more exceedingly an eternal weight of glory."[3] With these wonderful words Paul soars above all notion of controversy[4] with the Judaizers and wings his way to a height on the mountain far above cloud and storm. On this glory-crowned summit Paul stands serene and balances the affliction of his earthly ministry with the glory which is his. He is like one rapt in vision and probably dictates this sentence "fast and with beating heart."[5] He is interpreting his life and ministry in the light of the Cross and the light of the Risen and Glorious Christ.[6] Every word is here weighed against another. The affliction[7] is matched with the glory.[8] He does not so much minimize the affliction as magnify the glory. It matters little, the toil and stress by the way, now that the end is in sight. Standpoint

[1] 2 Tim. iv. 17.
[2] Phil. iv. 13.
[3] 2 Cor. iv. 17.
[4] Denney, *in loco.*
[5] Denney, *in loco.*
[6] Cf. Rev. v. 5 f.
[7] Cf. Rom. viii. 17.
[8] Cf. Rom. viii. 18.

determines much for us all. Paul is here looking at earth with heaven's eyes. If the telescope is turned round, the effect is very astonishing. What trifles our troubles will seem then! We can use Paul's eyes if we have difficulty in catching this view of life's values. The words "light"[1] and "weight"[2] stand over against each other. It is really "the lightness of the affliction."[3] He seems to hold the affliction in one hand and the glory in the other. The word for affliction suggests a heavy weight and glory seems intangible like a cloud, but things are not always what they seem. Jesus had said that His burden was light.[4] The glory seems to Paul actually like a heavy burden, so great and gracious it all is. The word for "weight" is the one used of those who bore the heat and burden of the day.[5] Once more, Paul drowns "for the moment"[6] in "eternal."[7] The notion is probably "present" in opposition with "future."[8] It will seem short from the point of view of eternity, but the affliction is confined to the "now-time," while the glory is perpetual with the unending future. There is no way to challenge

[1] Cf. Matt. xi. 30. [2] Burden. Cf. Gal. vi. 2.
[3] Classic idiom, article and neuter adjective like a substantive.
[4] Matt. xi. 30.
[5] Matt. xx. 12. The Hebrew word (Gen. xviii. 20; Job vi. 3) means both to be heavy and to be glorious.
[6] Here only in the New Testament.
[7] *Aionion.* [8] Meyer, Bernard.

the noble sentiment here expressed, if one holds to a belief in immortality. Paul does not mean that there is no glory in the ministry here. Far from it. But even if it were all tribulation, the glory to come would more than make amends. Thus one sees that the most of the minister's reward lies in the future, in the beyond, in the glory to be given by Jesus. That is the consolation of the true preacher. He does not enter the ministry to make money, to get honour, power, fame. Paul himself had turned his back on all the allurements of life when he surrendered to Christ on the way to Damascus. He is not in the least complaining now. He does not admit that the preacher should not have adequate remuneration. He often argued that he should.[1] But no salary could offer pay enough for the work of the ministry if that were all. Men to-day receive salaries of a hundred thousand dollars a year who are not comparable in character and worth as men for the real welfare of the world with ministers who do not receive a twentieth of that sum. A "trust" president gets all his pay in money. The minister receives most of his in glory, and most of that in the next world. But just this difference is all the difference between the material man and the spiritual man. The minister is entitled to a decent competency and

[1] Cf. I Cor. ix.

a church should be ashamed to stint the man who breaks to them the bread of life. But no amount of money could pay Paul for all that he had undergone. He did it "for Christ's sake," and Christ had not forgotten him. "The law of our humanity is life out of decay; the type and exemplification of which is the Cross of Christ. And this is the soother of affliction—this one steadfast thought—the glory which is being worked out thereby."[1] This is Paul's philosophy of trouble. It *works out*[2] the glory for us. "Except a grain of wheat fall into the earth and die, it abideth alone; but if it die, it beareth much fruit. He that loveth his life loseth it; and he that hateth his life in this world shall keep it unto life eternal. If any man serve Me, let him follow Me; and where I am, there shall also My servant be; if any man serve Me, him will the Father honour."[3] Affliction has glory as its fruit only when borne in the spirit of the Cross of Jesus. Trouble drives many to despair, to shame, to sensual excess and stupor, to death. "But go and tell him of the law *in Christ;* tell him that *He* has borne the Cross; and there is the peculiar Christian feeling of comfort, with all its tenderness, humanity, and *personality.*"[4] But Paul has not seen the whole of this mountain of glory—to change

[1] F. W. Robertson, "Life and Letters," p. 633.
[2] *Katergazetai.*
[3] John xii. 24–26.
[4] F. W. Robertson, "Life and Letters," p. 633.

his figure. The working goes on "more and more exceedingly."[1] He literally piles Ossa on Pelion in an effort to describe the vastness of the glory which is in store for him and every toiler for Christ. He loves to pile adverbs on top of adverbs like one big boulder on top of another in a riot of power.[2] There is the failure of language to compass the greatness of his conception. But the eye of faith can supply the rest.[3] Paul has expounded this interpretation of life elsewhere also with much power.[4]

3. *The Vision of the Unseen*

"While we look not at the things which are seen, but at the things which are not seen: for the things which are seen are temporal; but the things which are not seen are eternal."[5] Paul is looking[6] into the distance like a watchman peering far ahead. It is the calm triumphant contemplation of a conqueror. "We can well believe that the pressure was relaxed, and that the pen moved more steadily and slowly over the contemplative words that follow."[7] It is more than a glimpse or a momentary rhapsody of spiritual exaltation that Paul here means. It is the whole world-outlook[8] that is under consideration.

[1] From excess to excess. [2] Cf. Eph. iii. 20. [3] Cf. 1 Cor. ii. 9 f.
[4] Cf. Rom. viii. 26–39; Eph. iii. 14–21. [5] 2 Cor. iv. 18.
[6] Cf. Phil. iii. 14. [7] Denney, *in loco*. [8] *Welt-anschauung*.

No other standpoint will move the preacher to undergo the sacrifices to which he is called. Moses, whose glory Paul has been considering, chose rather to "share ill-treatment with the people of God, than to enjoy the pleasures of sin for a season; accounting the reproach of Christ greater riches than the treasures of Egypt; for he looked unto the recompense of reward. By faith he forsook Egypt, not fearing the wrath of the king: for he endured as seeing Him who is invisible."[1] These words seem written about Paul. Moses, the greatest man in the Jewish Dispensation, as the Jews counted greatness, was great just because, when God appeared to him at the Burning Bush, he recognized the Invisible God, and placed the Unseen above the seen. So he stood in the sands of Egypt and cast his lot with the people of God in their poverty and weakness and led them out and on through the wilderness towards the Land of Promise. And Paul too followed the gleam. Come what may, he is content. "Yea, and if I am offered upon the sacrifice of your faith, I joy, and rejoice with you all."[2] "I will most gladly spend and be spent for your souls."[3] It is not merely the power to see what is in the distance that is in Paul's mind, though that is true. The preacher should be able to look at life in its whole, not in a fragment or section. It is

[1] Heb. xi. 25–27. [2] Phil. ii. 17. [3] 2 Cor. xii. 15.

part, a large part, of the minister's work to help people to see things as they are, to brush away the cobwebs and the dust of business strife; to call men back to a just view of life. But there is more here than the future reward of eternal glory. Much that is unseen is invisible, from the nature of the case, in any material sense.[1] The soul is invisible, duty is invisible, principle is invisible, love is invisible. The greatest and best things are not seen nor handled. They are the things of the spirit. "Finally, brethren, whatsoever things are true, whatsoever things are honourable, whatsoever things are just, whatsoever things are pure, whatsoever things are lovely, whatsoever things are of good report; if there be any virtue, and if there be any praise, think on these things."[2] It is just because it is so hard for the average man to catch and keep this spiritual interpretation of life that the call is so great to-day for men of vision in the ministry. There is little use for any other sort. The seer is the man who tells what he has seen. The prophetic vision is essential to-day if ministers wish to grip and hold the consciences of men. The things that are seen[3] are temporary.[4] Out of the conflict of the nineteenth century the spiritual interpretation of the universe is triumphant. "In the

[1] F. W. Robertson, "Life and Letters," p. 633.
[2] Phil. iv. 8. [3] Cf. Rom. i. 20. [4] Cf. Heb. xi. 25.

beginning God." We come back to that. We start with God. The universe which we see with our eyes is merely the expression of God's will which we do not see with our eyes. As a matter of fact the invisible things are clearly seen with the mind's eye if the eye is open.[1] Paul is gazing at the eternal. He sees beyond the things of sense. He is a practical idealist. He is not, to be sure, using metaphysical terms in a fine-spun distinction between *noumena* and *phenomena*. He goes deeper than philosophical terms. His eye is on God and Christ. All else sinks out of sight, "looking unto Jesus the author and perfecter of our faith."[2] "Distrust of the supernatural, insistence on the present and the practical, and the pride of a self-styled common sense, have done much to rob Christianity of this vast horizon, to blind it to this heavenly vision."[3] It is all very well to decry too much "other-worldliness" on the part of impractical visionaries, but most men need this heavenly vision. We need our feet on the earth, but we should see the heavens opened. We are not going to make earth an Eden without the vision of Eden. All social reform should be linked on to the spiritual impulse, else it too will be transitory and pass away. When all other men clamour so much about time, the preacher may be allowed to call men

[1] Rom. i. 20. [2] Heb. xii. 2. [3] Denney, *in loco.*

to the contemplation of eternity and to a life here and now in view of eternity.

4. *The Earthly Tabernacle*

"For we know that if the earthly house of our tabernacle be dissolved, we have a building from God, a house not made with hands, eternal in the heavens."[1] These words bring Paul face to face with death as the outcome of his struggles. True, Jesus may come before death overtakes him. That is his sincere desire. He really groans[2] with a passionate longing[3] to be clothed upon[4] with the habitation[5] from heaven which will be his at the Second Coming of Christ without death, if he lives till then. This is the probable meaning of this mixture of metaphors which was natural to Paul since the tent cloth used by him in making tents was also used for garments.[6] As a matter of fact no single metaphor could express all that Paul wishes to say.[7] The new body at the Second Coming will come upon[8] the old without the decay of death. He is not anxious to drop the old, but to have the new.[9] Herodotus[10] tells of a Corinthian queen who, after death, appeared to her husband and asked him to burn dresses for

[1] 2 Cor. v. 1.
[2] 2 Cor. v. 2, 4.
[3] Cf. 2 Cor. ix. 14.
[4] Cf. John xxi. 7.
[5] Cf. Jude 6.
[6] Stanley, *in loco*. Cf. Psa. xciv. 2.
[7] Bernard, *in loco*.
[8] *Ependusasthai*.
[9] 2 Cor. v. 4.
[10] Herodotus, V. 92. Cf. Stanley, *in loco*.

her so that she may have clothing for her disembodied spirit. Paul has no such crude idea as that. "Knowledge and ignorance, doubt and certitude, are remarkably blended in these words. The apostle knows what many men are not certain of; the apostle doubts as to what all men now are certain of."[1] He is not certain[2] that he will die, for Jesus may come first. He is certain that, if death comes first, he has already the title to a heavenly body far more glorious than the earthly one. With measured words he balances the tent[3] which contains his spirit here on earth with the house[4] which will be his in heaven. His business as a tent-maker makes the metaphor very pertinent to Paul. The wanderings of the Israelites in the wilderness when they dwelt in tents on their way to the Promised Land also occur to one naturally. The tent is struck[5] at the breaking up of camp or by wind or storm. The tent is therefore temporary while the house is stable and eternal. The tent is on earth,[6] while the house from God is in heaven. The tent is tangible while the house is not made with hands as Paul made the tents of cloth. At every point death brings a blessing in

[1] Maclaren, "Expositions of Holy Scripture," *in loco*.
[2] Third class condition. Cf. Robertson, "Short Grammar of the Greek New Testament," p. 163.
[3] *Skenos*, not *skene*.
[4] *Oikia*.
[5] Torn down. Cf. Gal. ii. 18.
[6] Cf. Phil. ii. 10.

comparison with the earthly tabernacle of the Spirit. The note of confidence rings in Paul's words, "We know[1] that we have."[2] Let death do its worst and Paul is more than conqueror through Him that loves him.[3] There is perhaps an echo in Paul's memory of the wonderful lyric of the spiritual body in 1 Corinthians xv. 42–49. Paul does not despise the wonderful organism which he here calls a tent, but he justly understands that it is only the temporary abode of the eternal spirit which is to live with Christ in heaven.

5. *At Home With the Lord*

"We are of good courage, I say, and are willing rather to be absent from the body, and to be at home with the Lord."[4] Paul has a heavenly homesickness.[5] He feels in a sense absent[6] from the Lord. He is away from home and, gracious as are the wonderful glimpses of the Face of Christ which he has here, they will be far surpassed by the constant presence with Jesus in heaven. He is thinking of what it will be to be at home[7] with the Lord, to sit at the feet of Jesus and look Him in the face[8] to his heart's content, that wondrous face which looked at him on

[1] Clear conviction. [2] Present tense. [3] Rom. viii. 37.
[4] 2 Cor. v. 8. [5] Bernard, *in loco*.
[6] *Ekdemeo*. The Greek word occurs only in this passage in the New Testament.
[7] *Endemeo*. [8] *Pros*.

the Damascus road. Then what is mortal will be swallowed up of life.[1] He has even here and now the earnest[2] of the Spirit as a precious foretaste of what is in store for him. God wrought the joy of the present and God will bring the full fruition in His own good time. He has the conception of heaven that Jesus gives in John xiv. 1–3, that of home. There is no richer word than that. It is therefore with good courage[3] that Paul looks upon death as a friend rather than as a foe. It is not a cold river with Charon to row him over the dark waters. It is rather the portal to heaven, and Jesus stands at the door with outstretched hand to welcome the absent one home. He will many a time sigh for home and rest, to depart[4] and be with Christ. But, meanwhile, he is ready for work. He has no notion of folding his hands and doing nothing.[5] The "weight of glory" is an inspiration at the end of a full day's work, not an air-castle to take the place of duty here and now. Paul's other-worldliness took the form of making him more aggressive against all sin and wrong in this world.

[1] 2 Cor. v. 4. [2] Cf. 2 Cor. i. 22. [3] 2 Cor. v. 6, 8.
[4] Cf. Phil. i. 23. [5] Cf. Phil. i. 24–26.

VII

WELL PLEASING UNTO HIM—THE PREACHER'S MASTER PASSION

(*2 Cor. v. 9–21*)

"Wherefore we make it our aim, whether at home or absent, to be well pleasing unto Him."

—*2 Cor. v. 9.*

VII

WELL PLEASING UNTO HIM—THE PREACHER'S MASTER PASSION

1. *Paul's Ambition*

"WE are ambitious to be well pleasing unto Him."[1] Come life, come death, Paul's ambition was one and the same. Ambition is a word in ill-repute. It comes from the Latin *ambo*, both. The Roman politicians, eager to get office, could get on both sides of a proposition, to curry favour with the people. They would face both ways at once. It was applied to a man who would go any lengths to carry his selfish ends. But there is a good side to the word, bad as the origin of the English word is. The Greek[2] word has a much nobler origin. It means to be fond of honour. One is actuated by a love of honour to strive for noble ends. Paul exhorts the Thessalonians to be ambitious to be quiet.[3] He is himself ambitious to preach the Gospel where other men have not been so as not to build upon another man's foundation.[4] With Paul it is a matter of honour[5] to please Christ.

[1] 2 Cor. v. 9.
[2] *Philo-timeomai.*
[3] 1 Thess. iv. 11.
[4] Rom. xv. 20.
[5] Meyer, *in loco.*

Surely this is a perfectly legitimate ambition.[1] Since he surrendered to Christ that has been the master motive of his life, to be well pleasing to Him. This deep undertone comes to the surface often in his Epistles.[2] He is like the musician who cares naught for the applause of the audience if he can catch the eye of approval from the master who taught him. He is under orders and his constant aim is to please his great taskmaster. "He that judgeth me is the Lord."[3] Paul brought "every thought into captivity to the obedience of Christ."[4] He stands entranced by the meekness and gentleness of Christ.[5] There is no comfort in Paul for the nerveless, spineless minister who is afraid of his shadow, who runs at a whisper, who lacks virility, who speaks peace when there is no peace, who is satisfied with things as they are, who watches for the praise of the groundlings, who trims his sail to every wind that blows, who caters to popular taste, however maudlin and sensational. The minister without ambition will accomplish nothing for God or man, only let his ambition not be the feverish restlessness to get another man's place and an unwillingness to do a full man's work where he is. Here is a true word:[6] "He will make but a poor

[1] "*Hæc una ambitio legitima*," Bengel.
[2] Rom. xii. 1 f.; xiv. 18; Eph. v. 10; Phil. iv. 18; Col. iii. 10; Tit. ii. 9.
[3] 1 Cor. iv. 4. [4] 2 Cor. x. 5. [5] 2 Cor. x. 1.
[6] Stalker, "The Preacher and His Models," p. 207.

minister who would not be an earnest worker for God and man, even if he were not a minister." There are few preachers who do not have a sporadic ambition to please Christ. The trouble is to hold one's self to this high ideal year in and year out. So many complications will arise, so many interruptions to one's work, so rapidly the time slips by. The sermon does not get the work that it ought to have. The visits are not made that are clamouring for attention. The work does not get on. A fresh look at the Unwearied Christ will spur one on to the best and the highest. The child comes to the father for approval of his toy. The minister will one day meet Christ who will inspect his work. Praise is sweet, but the praise from Christ will be sweetest of all, if He says: "Well done, good and faithful servant; enter thou into the joy of thy Lord."

2. *The Judgment-Seat of Christ*

"For we must all be made manifest before the judgment-seat of Christ."[1] This solemn outlook is not confined to preachers. Paul has been using the literary plural freely, but here he is careful to include "all."[2] The point to press is that ministers are in no wise exempt. The *Bema*[3] was a lofty seat at the

[1] 2 Cor. v. 10.
[2] All, both living and dead.
[3] Cf. Stanley, *in loco*.

end of the Basilica on a high platform. The judge could thus be seen towering above the crowd. The more common figure for the judgment is a throne.[1] But this is a most impressive picture.[2] Jesus had claimed[3] to be the Judge and Paul understands that fact clearly. Part of the penalty for sin is the confirmation in sin. Each one receives[4] the things done in the body. In this sense God's punishments are not arbitrary, but are the inevitable development of the man's real self.[5] "Whatsoever a man soweth, that shall he also reap."[6] "And he that is filthy, let him be made filthy still."[7] The key-word in Paul's word in 2 Corinthians v. 10 is "made manifest."[8] We must be made manifest, like an open book, right in the presence[9] of Christ. The white light of eternal truth will beat down upon us and our works. Paul describes[10] the pitiful plight of those religious teachers who will themselves be saved so as by fire, but the whole fabric of their life-work and teaching will be burned up like wood, hay, or stubble. There is no reward to the preacher who builds with that sort of material. The ordeal of fire is before the work of

[1] Cf. Matt. xxv. 31; Rev. xx. 11.
[2] Cf. Rom. xiv. 10.
[3] Matt. xxv. 31 ff.; xxvi. 64.
[4] Gets back in full.
[5] Cf. F. W. Robertson, "Life and Letters," p. 639.
[6] Gal. vi. 7.
[7] Rev. xxii. 11. "In this world we have not seen the last of anything." Denney, *in loco*.
[8] From *phaneros*.
[9] *Emprosthen*.
[10] 1 Cor. iii. 12–15.

every preacher and Christian. Indeed, so solemn is Paul's sense of responsibility as a preacher of the Gospel that he buffeted[1] his body "lest by any means, after I have preached to others, I myself should be rejected."[2] He took no chances with his own soul. "Ministers of the Gospel have become Papists, infidels, freethinkers, and plotted the destruction of what they once professed to prize. We may be apostles, and yet, like Judas, turn out to be sons of perdition. Woe unto us if this be the case."[3] John Owen pungently said: "No man preaches his sermon well to others if he doth not first preach it to his own heart." With preachers as with all men "the pathos of life is the disproportion betwen the promise and the reality."[4] There is truth in what Forsyth[5] says: "The deadliest Pharisaism is not hypocrisy; it is the unconscious Pharisaism of unreality." The result of this tremendous responsibility is not to dissuade a man from entering the ministry, but to incite him to his noblest endeavour for Christ's sake. To shirk the call of duty is to incur the penalty of cowardice, which is loss of self-respect and the lashing of conscience. At any rate we must all stand beside[6] the

[1] Cf. Luke xviii. 5. [2] 1 Cor. ix. 27.
[3] Spurgeon, "Lectures to Students," Second Series, p. 43.
[4] Hoyt, "The Preacher," p. 24.
[5] "Positive Preaching and the Modern Mind," p. 175.
[6] Cf. Rom. xiv. 10.

judgment-seat of God in the end of the day. "And there is no creature that is not manifest in His sight: but all things are naked and laid open before the eyes of Him with whom we have to do."[1] The goal before us all is to please Jesus who is our chief Helper and Friend in His work. Epicurus wrote to his friend: "I tell this not to the world but to thee; for we are a great enough theatre one to the other." On this Dr. David Smith[2] comments: "And the Presence of Jesus is our Theatre. The King is in the audience, and His eye is upon us. He is observing how we comport ourselves upon the stage, and before His Face we dare not play an ignoble part. His commendation is enough."

3. *Persuading Men*

"We persuade men."[3] Paul probably means, "we try to persuade men."[4] He is successful with some, but not with all. At Athens some mocked.[5] At Rome Paul spent a whole day persuading the Jews concerning Jesus. Some believed, and some disbelieved.[6] One incentive before Paul at this moment is the fear of the Lord. With the judgment-seat of Christ in mind he seeks to be faithful to the men of his generation. He is sure that God understands

[1] Heb. iv. 13.
[2] "The Face of Jesus," p. 46.
[3] 2 Cor. v. 11.
[4] Conative present.
[5] Acts xvii. 32.
[6] Acts xxviii. 23 f.

him and he hopes that the consciences[1] of the Corinthians approve the sincerity and faithfulness of his ministry. Paul's knowledge of the terror of the Lord made him zealous to persuade men. He was no rhetorical thunderer about the horrors of hell who went home with zest unimpaired.[2] "We must regain our sense of *soul* greatness, and our sense of its eternal price."[3] In the "Memoirs of Dr. Chalmers"[4] there is an extract from his diary which is a revelation of his great spirit in his attitude towards the work of the ministry. "Prayed for knowledge, for the understanding and impression and remembrance of God's Word; for growth in grace, for personal holiness, for that sanctification which the redeemed undergo. Thought of the sins that most easily beset me; confessed them, and prayed for correction and deliverance. They are—anxiety about worldly matters, when any suspicion or uncertainty attaches to them; a disposition to brood over provocations; impatience at the irksome peculiarities of others; an industriousness from a mere principle of animal activity, without the glory of God and the service of mankind lying at the bottom of it; and above all, a taste and an appetite for human applause. My con-

[1] 2 Cor. v. 11.
[2] F. W. Robertson, "Life and Letters," p. 640.
[3] Forsyth, "Positive Preaching and the Modern Mind," p. 174.
[4] Vol. I, p. 288.

science smote me on the subject of pulpit exhibitions. I pray that God may make usefulness the grand principle of my appearances there. Read the promises annexed to faithful ministers, and prayed for zeal, diligence, and ability in the discharge of my ministerial office. Prayed for the people, individually for some, and generally for all descriptions of them. Prayed for friends individually, and relations. Read the promises relative to the progress of the Gospel and conversion of the Jews. Prayed for those objects." It is with this spirit that one is able to be all things to all men[1] if by all means he may save some. The aim of one's ministry is the conversion of men and the training of their souls. The evangelistic and teaching ministry need to be combined. There is a tendency to-day to underrate the sermon. "The sermon is the climax of public worship. It summons to the throne of God a larger number of faculties than any other act of worship. It calls upon everything within to bless God's holy name."[2] The sermon needs to be magnified, not discounted. But one must remember also that one's "own tone, temper, and spirit in preaching"[3] have a deal to do with the conversion of sinners. The problem of every minister is how to make both his preaching and life effect-

[1] 1 Cor. ix. 22.
[2] Jefferson, "The Building of the Church," p. 281.
[3] Spurgeon, "Lectures to Students," Second Series, p. 277.

ive in winning men to Christ. The Gospel remains the same in its essential content, but men of every age have fresh difficulties which have to be met by a new appropriation and application of the Gospel of Christ. It is not enough to know the Bible and other books. The preacher must have a sympathetic knowledge of the men whom he is to persuade.[1] "Each man begins his destiny where the first babe began, in old sorrows and sadness; and continues it in old sins and sores."[2] In the work of persuasion the minister will find men who put hindrances in the way of his work.[3] It will help little to lose one's temper in such case.

4. *Beside Ourselves*

"For whether we are beside ourselves, it is unto God."[4] Some of the friends, possibly members of His own household, had once thought Jesus beside Himself.[5] John the Baptist was accused of having a demon[6] because he was ascetic and abstemious in his habits. Jesus was called gluttonous and a wine-bibber because He was not ascetic.[7] The Pharisees explained the works of Jesus as wrought by the devil.[8]

[1] Cf. Phelps, "Men and Books," p. 3.
[2] Armitage, "Preaching," p. 145.
[3] Parker, "Ad Clerum," p. 207 f.
[4] 2 Cor. v. 13.
[5] Mark iii. 21.
[6] Matt. xi. 18. Cf. Robertson, "John the Loyal," p. 199.
[7] Matt. xi. 19.
[8] Matt. xii. 24.

In a frenzy of rage they say that He is a Samaritan and has a demon.[1] Paul probably is thinking of his enemies in Corinth who had apologized for him by saying that he was not responsible.[2] The very visions which Paul had had may have been turned against him as proof of his erratic mentality.[3] He admits ironically that he is playing the fool in boasting of himself as they had compelled him to do.[4] He may be here alluding to the charge made against him that he was a fool. The very earnestness of Paul concerning the cause of Christ in Corinth was used by his enemies as proof as his lack of balance. He could be passionate in speech as is shown by the effect of his address on Festus who exclaims in a loud voice: "Paul, thou art mad; thy much learning is turning thee mad."[5] It is one of the commonest of charges against zealous ministers that they are a little "off." It is one of the keenest weapons of the devil with which to clip the wings of a preacher's power. "The disciple and the Master alike seemed to those who did not understand them to be in an overstrained, too highly-wrought condition of spirit."[6] Paul does not care to deny that he had lost himself in his zeal for God. He had a real enthusiasm,[7] God in him. A God-filled man seems crazy to a dead

[1] John viii. 48.
[2] Cf. our word "ecstasy."
[3] 2 Cor. xii. 1–7.
[4] 2 Cor. xi. 1–17.
[5] Acts xxvi. 24.
[6] Denney, *in loco.*
[7] *Enthousiasmos.*

man of the world. Life seems derangement to death. Paul could speak with tongues[1] and that fact may also have been used against him. So far as Paul was concerned, he did not care. It was "to God," for the glory of God, in the cause of God. Better far have a holy *abandon* for God than too much icy reserve, "icily regular, splendidly null." Dr. A. C. Dixon says that a graveyard is the most dignified place on earth. A man and a church can have too much dignity to be of any use. Paul is willing to be considered beside himself. The preacher is discounted as peculiar if he does not join in all the follies and sins of modern society. He is damned as a worldling if he does. Paul met the counter criticism also. Some thought that he was too soberminded.[2] He was too crafty and worldly-wise; "being crafty I caught you with guile,"[3] they charged. He had sent Titus after their money for the poor saints, that is, Paul. If a minister saves a little money for his family, he is sure to be called mercenary by some. Probably different enemies brought the different accusations. But they do not really believe what they say. They talk with the face, not with the heart.[4] It is often the case that men ridicule preachers just because they are public characters,

[1] 1 Cor. xiv. 14–18.
[2] 2 Cor. v. 13.
[3] 2 Cor. xii. 16.
[4] 2 Cor. v. 12.

just to see if they can be provoked into doing or saying foolish things or just to provoke their friends to anger. The prophet is often held to be beside himself. They will burn Savonarola in Florence and coming generations will build his monument. In Oxford the monument stands to Cranmer, Ridley and Latimer. The ashes of Wycliff may have gone to the sea in the waters of the Severn, but the English people have the Bible in their vernacular. Paul challenges the Corinthians to take either horn of the dilemma. If he was prudent, it was for their sakes; if he was beside himself, it was for God.[1] Paul has "a continuous sense of the infinite."[2] It is easy for a preacher to be full of himself or of the current ideas. The sermon will be "after all only a lecture or a leading article."[3] "I went longing to hear about Christ, and it was only Newman from beginning to end."[4] If the preacher allows the critical faculty to crucify spiritual passion, all the finesse of overrefinement and exactitude will not atone for the absence of soul and passion. "It is the flash of the spirit and not the words of the lips which is the best thing which a great man has to give. Catch that and you have an imperishable possession. To feel upon one's life the hot breath of a great heart, to

[1] F. W. Robertson, "Life and Letters," p. 692.
[2] Beecher, "Yale Lectures on Preaching," Third Series, p. 321.
[3] Moule, "To My Younger Brethren," p. 259. [4] *Ibid.*

drink into one's being the life of a great soul in one of its great moments, is a privilege which does not come often and which should be valued above rubies and fine gold."[1] Spirit is fused with spirit in the holy passion of that fire.

5. *The Grip of Christ's Love*

"For the love of Christ constraineth us."[2] They may think him crafty or crazy. It is a small matter to Paul. He has caught a vision of Christ's love for him as shown by His death for us all.[3] There is no denying the central place in his theology which Paul here gives to the death of Christ. He died for our sakes and rose again[4] to prove His power to save from sin. We who have been saved by Christ no longer belong to ourselves. We are to live unto Christ. That in brief is Paul's conception of his own relation to Jesus. He is the bond-slave of Christ purchased by the blood of Christ. The love of that Christ as thus shown holds Paul captive to the end. The word "constrain"[5] is a bold one. It is used of those in the grip[6] of various diseases. Peter's mother-in-law was held[7] in the power of a fever. The Gadarenes were seized[8] with great fear when

[1] Jefferson, "The Building of the Church," p. 292.
[2] 2 Cor. v. 14. [3] 2 Cor. v. 14. [4] 2 Cor. v. 15.
[5] Literally holds together. [6] Matt. iv. 24.
[7] Luke iv. 38. [8] Luke viii. 37.

they saw what Christ had done to the demoniac. The multitudes press[1] Jesus together almost to suffocation. Jesus felt the pressure[2] in His spirit till His baptism of blood be received. When Stephen told of seeing Jesus standing at the right hand of God, the Sanhedrin held[3] their hands over their ears. When Timothy and Silas came to Corinth from Thessalonica Paul held himself[4] continuously to the word of preaching. Paul later felt himself in a strait[5] betwixt two whether to stay or depart and be with Christ. These are the chief New Testament examples of this word. The love of Christ holds Paul fast. "O love that will not let me go." In a sense, Paul has no choice, since, as in a vice, he is held fast by the love of Christ.[6] It is more than the categorical imperative of duty. It is the magnet of love that is irresistible, once you have yielded yourself to its power. The mother is the slave of her sick child.[7] She cannot help herself if she have a mother's heart. But this high pressure together[8] creates a mighty propulsion and energy. The constraint is not restraint. It is impulse.[9] The boiler that holds the steam makes possible the onward pressure that drives the engine and pulls the train. The love of Christ

[1] Luke viii. 45.
[2] Luke xii. 50.
[3] Acts vii. 57.
[4] Acts xviii. 5.
[5] Phil. i. 23.
[6] Denney, *in loco.*
[7] F. W. Robertson, "Life and Letters," p. 644.
[8] *Sun.*
[9] "*Urget nos,*" Vulgate.

presses me hard, harasses[1] me so that I have no rest save in pushing on for Christ. Christ's love lets me have no peace.[2] In this word, then, Paul has revealed the master-passion of his ministry. He has no desire to get beyond Christ. Jesus is ever with him and ever lures him on to higher heights. With unwearied tread Paul presses on towards the goal. In his darkest hours he hears the footfall of Christ at his side: "Be not afraid, but speak and hold not thy peace: for I am with thee, and no man shall set on thee to harm thee."[3] To Paul Christ was all and in all.[4] He does not look on Christ as he once did, as the Jews do now, "after the flesh."[5] He has gone far beyond that stage, he is glad to say. The new view of Christ has made a new world for Paul. He looks at everything from a new angle of vision. He has a new motive in life, a new passion, a new outlook. The gold is not at the end of the rainbow for him. He has found the secret of real life. It is Christ.

6. *The New View of Man*

"Wherefore we henceforth know no man after the flesh."[6] The reason is that Paul himself is a new man[7] in Christ Jesus. "The old things are passed

[1] Ewald.
[2] Chrysostom.
[3] Acts xviii. 9f. Cf. Acts xxiii. 11.
[4] Col. iii. 11.
[5] 2 Cor. v. 16.
[6] 2 Cor. v. 16.
[7] 2 Cor. v. 17.

away; behold, they are become new."[1] The ancient order of prejudice and hate has gone. In its place has come the new love for man of whatever race. In Christ Jesus there is neither Greek nor Jew, circumcision nor uncircumcision, Barbarian nor Scythian, bond nor free.[2] The middle wall of partition between Jew and Gentile was broken down, but it was done only by the Cross of Christ.[3] Paul feels himself debtor both to Greek and Barbarian.[4] It is the crowning glory of Paul's ministry that to him was given the grace of telling the unsearchable riches of Christ to the Gentiles.[5] The point to get hold of is that this was a complete revolution in the ancient world. Jews and Samaritans hated each other. Greeks despised the barbarous outsiders. The proud Romans scorned those whom they conquered. There was an impassable social gulf between master and slave. The love of man as man, the notion that "a man's a man for a' that," was foreign to the ancient world. Christ discovered the worth of the individual man and formed the first real democracy, that of the spirit. Paul made this discovery in Christ. "Democracy was born at Bethlehem—not, as Carlyle declared, at Bunker's Hill. And the spiritual movement towards democracy is very far indeed

[1] 2 Cor. v. 17.
[2] Col. iii. 11.
[3] Eph. ii. 14 f.
[4] Rom. i. 14.
[5] Eph. iii. 8.

from complete."[1] Perpetua and Felicitos, though matron and slave, clasp hands as Christian martyrs. Christianity alone can break down the caste system of India. Even the Christian world is very far from having grasped clearly the significance of what Jesus has done for man. But Paul saw it. He was a new man himself. Paul has new eyes with which to look upon the world, the eyes of Jesus which had looked in pity upon him. He has a new heart of love for men. Jesus has made a new world for Paul. The passion for souls that spurs the missionary to heroic endeavour to uplift the race is grounded in the love of Christ. The worth of man is recognized in its fullness only in the light of the Cross. The world is in a state of flux. There are always modern problems for the modern man, but this does not mean that Christians must drop the gospel view of man. As a matter of fact what modern Christianity most needs to do is to come up to Christ's view of man and apply it to the actual social problems of to-day in harmony with the love of Christ, but not with the bald literalism of Tolstoi.[2] Evolution has thrown new light on our knowledge of man and the world-order, but evolution has not wrought such a revolu-

[1] W. Robertson Nicoll, *British Weekly*, Jan. 19, 1911.
[2] Cf. Matthews, "The Church and the Changing Order"; "The Gospel and the Modern Man."

tion in man's view of man as has Christianity.[1] As to the revolution in Paul's own mind it is just the contrast between Saul the Pharisee and Paul the Apostle to the Gentiles.[2] He does not mean [3] that, as a Christian, he once shared the narrow prejudices of the Jews which he has since outgrown. He grew constantly in his apprehension of Christ's love and so in appreciation of man, but it was all along the new turn made in his life by Jesus. The old Jewish rabbinical views of the Messiah and of Jewish exclusiveness vanished. A new order has come.[4] The death of Christ marked a new epoch in the history of the human race. "Had he foreseen distinctly that a new era would be dated from that time; that a new society, philosophy, literature, moral code, would grow up from it over continents of which he knew not the existence; he could not have more strongly expressed his sense of the greatness of the event than in what is here said."[5] He had himself never apparently seen Jesus in the flesh, but he knows Him in the spirit and he understands the moral and spiritual revolution wrought by Jesus. It is the greatest of all time, this new love for man as the offspring of God, this new sense of the brotherhood of the race

[1] Cf. Orr, "The Christian View of God and the World as Centering in the Incarnation."
[2] Bernard, *in loco.*
[3] B. Jowett, *in loco.*
[4] Cf. Isa. xliii. 18 f.; Heb. viii. 13.
[5] Stanley, *in loco.*

that calls for the best that is in a man to be given freely as an offering for men.[1] The touch-stone that makes this "new world"[2] is Christ. "In Christ"[3] all men meet on a common level and are made new creatures. I have just seen the lantern slides of life in Burmah and India given by Dr. Vinton, missionary in Burmah. The most striking thing is the expression on the faces of children and grown men and women after they become Christians. Positively it looks like a miracle, so great is the transformation in the eye and the whole countenance.[4] Indeed, it is the constant miracle of God's grace. There is inexpressible power and appeal in Jesus Christ to find the good that is left in man after the ruin of sin and link on to that and transform the heart and life by the Holy Spirit. The old prophets dimly saw the glory in the Messiah of whom they spoke.[5] A painter stood before a masterpiece of a genius and felt the uplift of spirit as he humbly said: "And I too am a painter." The power of Christ is as great to-day as when He looked upon Simon and threw the spell of His spirit upon him.[6] Instead of being crushed by the sense of our unworthiness as we look at Jesus we are lifted up with the ineffable hope that this is what

[1] Phil. ii. 17. [2] Denney, *in loco.* [3] *En Christo.*
[4] Cf. also Begbie's "Twice-Born Men." The British edition of this book is called "Broken Earthenware."
[5] 1 Peter i. 11. [6] John i. 42.

we ought to be like, what we will try to be like.[1] We can never get away from Christ. Intellectual unrest will give place to spiritual aspiration.[2]

7. *The Ministry of Reconciliation*

"And gave unto us the ministry of reconciliation . . . having committed unto us the word of reconciliation."[3] This is a great word that Paul uses here. Nothing that can ever be said of the ministry lifts it to a higher plane than the service of reconciliation. But we are not to mistake our calling. Ministers are not priests in the sense that we have to propitiate God. It is true that there was estrangement on God's part towards sin. God is represented as angry with sin. He punishes sin. God is bound to punish willful sin against Himself.[4] "There is something in God as well as something in man that has to be dealt with before there can be peace. Nay, the something on God's side is so incomparably more serious in comparison with it that the something on man's side simply passes out of view. It is God's earnest dealing with the obstacle

[1] F. W. Robertson, "Life and Letters," p. 652.

[2] Cf. Selbie, "Aspects of Christ," p. 270. See also "Religion and the Modern Mind," and "Religion and the Modern World."

[3] 2 Cor. v. 18 f.

[4] F. W. Robertson, "Life and Letters," p. 656. "It was Christ's work to reconcile God to man. That is done, and done forever; we cannot add anything to it. That is a priestly power; and it is at our peril that we claim such a power."

on His own side to peace with man which prevails on man to believe in the seriousness of His love, and to lay aside distrust."[1] But God has met His problem in a way satisfactory to Himself. He has found a way by which to remain just and to justify the sinner.[2] The whole wonderful adjustment[3] is of God's love.[4] "All things are of God."[5] We may leave with God, as Paul does, God's side of the matter, except to accent the fact that in Christ we see God reconciling the world to Himself.[6] This is the sublime spectacle in the life and death of Christ. The Cross is God's overture to man for pardon and peace,[7] "not reckoning unto them their trespasses."[8] We have the picture of God endeavouring[9] to reconcile the world to Himself through Christ. The love of God prompts the whole effort. Christ is the Mediator between God and man.[10] It is precisely at this point that the minister of Christ comes in. He must speak the word of reconciliation to those who otherwise will not know of God's love and pardon in Christ or who, if they know, will not heed. It is a work worthy of angels, yea, of the Son of God Himself who Himself was the greatest Preacher of the Gospel. Jesus best interpreted to men His own

[1] Denney, *in loco*.
[2] Rom. iii. 26.
[3] *Katallage.*
[4] John iii. 16.
[5] 2 Cor. v. 18.
[6] Cf. Meyer and Bachmann.
[7] Eph. ii. 15 ff.
[8] 2 Cor. v. 19.
[9] Conative participle.
[10] 1 Tim. ii. 5.

mission and work. The Holy Spirit is promised as the teacher of those who are to set forth the work of Christ to men. "He shall glorify Me: for He shall take of Mine, and shall declare it unto you."[1] No minister can present Christ as the World's Reconciler to God without the help of the Holy Spirit whom God is anxious to bestow.[2] The minister is the interpreter of Christ to men in order to win men back to God, to make peace in their hearts with God. There is no earthly task so delicate and fraught with such results in time and eternity. The sermon is nothing in itself if it does not contribute towards this end. The pastoral visits, the gifts, the machinery of church life go for naught if they do not help on the work of winning men back to God. This is the work of God in Christ in the world. All else is subsidiary to this. We are God's coworkers in this great enterprise.[3] "A sermon is the life-blood of a Christian spirit. A preacher dies in the act of preaching. He lays down his life for his brethren. He saves others, himself he cannot save. The pulpit is a Golgotha in which the preacher gives his life for the life of the world."[4] The message of the preacher is that of his Master: "Be ye reconciled to God."[5] Paul is a preacher of God's peace and an exhorter of peace to men.

[1] John xvi. [2] Luke xi. 13. [3] 1 Cor. iii. 9.
[4] Jefferson, "The Building of the Church," p. 287. [5] 2 Cor. v. 20.

8. *Ambassadors for Christ*

"We are ambassadors therefore on behalf of Christ, as though God were entreating by us."[1] The word for being an ambassador is one of great dignity.[2] It is common among the ancient writers. In Luke xiv. 32 Jesus tells of one king who, "while the other is yet a great way off, sendeth an embassage, and asketh conditions of peace."[3] Paul is fully conscious of the great commission which he bears from God on behalf of Christ. In a word Paul, as all ministers are, is God's spokesman to men. He comes with authoritative word as the ambassador from the Court of Heaven to plead the cause of Christ with men whom God so loved that He gave His Son to die for them. He has a word for the rebellious Corinthians: "We beseech you on behalf of Christ."[4] It is surely a remarkable proof of God's love that He sends forth ambassadors to beg[5] men to receive His pardon in Christ for their sins. The utter sinfulness of human nature is revealed in the perversity that makes this necessary. An earnest ministry is one thoroughly convinced of the reality of sin. Paul feels his own need of prayer with such a task committed to him. He asks that prayer be made for him "that utterance may be given unto me

[1] 2 Cor. v. 20. [2] Meyer. [3] Cf. also Luke xix. 14.
[4] 2 Cor. v. 20. [5] *Deometha.*

in opening my mouth, to make known with boldness the mystery of the Gospel, for which I am an ambassador in chains; that I may speak boldly, as I ought to speak."[1] He is still Christ's ambassador though wearing a chain.[2] No ambassador in Rome wore a ring with more pride than Paul came to feel towards that chain. The value of the individual preacher is "truth plus personality."[3] It is no wonder that Paul felt acutely the peril in his own personality. The effectiveness of the gospel message inevitably varies with the changing personality of the preacher. "A man's personality is not a fixed and unchanging element. At any moment it is the resultant of what he has received and done."[4] Dr. Hoyt considers Phillips Brooks "the richest personality in the history of the modern pulpit, the strongest teacher of the fact that preaching is truth through personality." But the same point is borne out by a study of other great preachers.[5] The best of ministers have their "Fainting Fits" as Spurgeon called them. "Poor human nature cannot bear such strains as heavenly triumphs bring to it; there must come a reaction. Excess of joy as excitement must be paid for by

[1] Eph. vi. 19 f.
Literally "in a chain."
[3] Phillips Brooks.
[4] Hoyt, "The Preacher," p. 27.
[5] Cf. Broadus, "History of Preaching"; Ker, "History of Preaching"; Dargan, "History of Preaching"; Brastow, "Representative Modern Preachers"; Wilkinson, "Modern Masters of Pulpit Discourse."

subsequent depressions. . . . Whirled off our feet by a revival, carried aloft by popularity, exalted by success in soul-winning, we should be as the chaff which the wind driveth away, were it not that the gracious discipline of mercy breaks the ships of our vainglory with a strong east wind, and casts us shipwrecked, naked and forlorn, upon the Rock of Ages."[1] In this respect, as in much else, Paul is a model for the modern minister.[2] The courage in Paul is not due to a conviction of his own superior qualifications for his task, but rather to the fullness of the work of Christ. He has a full salvation to offer to men. "Him who knew no sin He made to be sin on our behalf."[3] This is the heart of the atoning death and work of Christ. Paul's clear grip on this great truth gives him solidity and positiveness. God's purpose is that we ourselves may become in Christ the righteousness of God. Thus there shall come to pass real righteousness in our lives. A redeemed humanity will become a sanctified humanity in Christ. Paul never gets out of sight of Christ. He is Christ's Ambassador. He must make his report to Christ. He is to appear at the judgment-seat of Christ. He longs to be well pleasing to Christ. Meanwhile the love of Christ holds him

[1] Spurgeon, "Lectures to Students," First Series, p. 257 f.
[2] Cf. Wilkinson, "Modern Masters of Pulpit Discourse," p. 523.
[3] 2 Cor. v. 21.

steadily to his ministry of reconciliation to bring on the new order in the world, the order of peace towards God, of love, of the reign of God in the hearts of men. Moreover, the world loves the preacher who takes his calling seriously, who is in deadly earnest. This does not mean that the preacher must be out of touch with men. The tremendous sense of his high calling rests largely on the worth of men. They are worth saving. They were worth Christ's dying for them. They are worth our living for them.

VIII

IN GLORY AND DISHONOUR—TAKING LIFE AS IT IS

(*2 Cor. vi. 1–10*)

> " By glory and dishonour, by evil report and good report."
>
> —*2 Cor. vi. 8.*

VIII

IN GLORY AND DISHONOUR—TAKING LIFE AS IT IS

1. *Working Together With Him*

"AND working together with Him."[1] Paul is a coworker with God, "for we are God's fellow workers."[2] God is the worker and Paul is the coworker. That is his glory and the secret of success in the ministry. The stars in their courses fight for the man who is partner with God in the world's redemption. Modern science has taught us the wisdom of following the ways of nature. They are God's ways. But God has not revealed all of Himself in nature. His heart is manifested in Christ Jesus. Just as the scientist laboriously delves into the secrets of nature to learn her processes and plans, so the minister of God must learn the plan of God in Christ as unfolded in His Word and in His dealings with men. He must know the ways of the soul and of God's spirit. In the work of rescuing men we can only follow the lead of God in Christ. God is a patient workman.[3] "And it takes Him all

[1] 2 Cor. vi. 1.

[2] 1 Cor. iii. 9.

[3] Maclaren, "Expositions," *in loco.*

His energies, for all a lifetime, to prepare His child for what He wants to make of him."[1] Paul is an ambassador, but he is also a builder, a teacher, a worker in the Lord's field. The preacher is first an evangelist, then a teacher.[2] But the minister's work is only begun when he has led a soul to Christ. If the first thought here seems to be the power of God with whom the minister works, one must not overlook the other side. Paul is really speaking of himself as *working* in connection with God. It is God who gives cheer and success, but the minister must *work* all the more because God is his Partner in the work of the kingdom. There is no blessing promised to the lazy or careless or self-satisfied preacher. "The higher classes no less resolutely than the lower withhold their spirit of obeisance from any man who is too good for it, too refined, too scholarly, too gentlemanly, or too indolent and too weak. The preacher, therefore, who has no power with the common people, has, in fact, no power with anybody. The pulpit which has no standing ground down in the lowlands of society has none anywhere. An exclusive ministry is always a weak ministry."[3] Paul is himself a noble example of how a man of the finest sensibilities and culture can adapt his ministry to all

[1] Maclaren, "Expositions," *in loco.*
[2] Denney, *in loco.*
[3] Phelps, "Men and Books," p. 69.

classes. He is able to be intellectually alert and alive to all the pressing doctrinal issues of a vital Christianity in its grapple with the theological vagaries and philosophy of the time.[1] But Paul knows how to be a man of affairs in the work of leadership[2] in the churches without any diminution of spiritual power. He is practical to the last degree in all the details of the collection for the poor saints at Jerusalem.[3] He shows consummate generalship in the conference at Jerusalem when he wins a decisive victory over the Judaizers.[4] There is no taint of obscurantism in Paul and he compromises no truth in his championship of freedom. He is anxious that Timothy may be "a workman that needeth not to be ashamed, handling aright the word of truth."[5] Thus he will be approved unto God. It is entirely possible for a man to dull his spiritual sensibilities in the mere details of church finance and church business and thus lose the richer results of his life-work. "The quiet country minister who trained an Alexander Duff into the faith and purpose of a missionary may have done more for the kingdom of God than many a man who has had thousands hanging on his

[1] Cf. his conflict with the Judaizers in 2 Corinthians and Galatians and with incipient Gnosticism in Colossians and Ephesians.
[2] Cf. Mott, "The Future Leadership of the Church."
[3] Cf. 2 Cor. viii. and ix.
[4] Acts xv.; Gal. ii.
[5] 2 Tim. ii. 15.

word. We need a spiritual vision of work as well as of the truth."[1] There is cheer in this contemplation for many a devoted minister whose name is not prominent in the press. But he may outrank some of the popular idols when the rewards are distributed. The measure of a minister's work is not the noise made by the rattle of the machinery. The noise often shows that the machinery is out of order and needs oiling. "The Church's worship, which should gather and greaten its soul, is sacrificed to its work. You have bustle all the week and baldness on Sunday. You have energy everywhere except in the spirit."[2] Paul was serene in the conviction of the present power of the Risen Christ.[3] There is no offhand patent guarantee for a successful ministry as men count success. What seems to us a highly successful work may be quite otherwise in God's eye. Joseph Parker discourses brilliantly on "The Guarantees of a Successful Ministry."[4] He has a sane word in this: "Our work in the ministry will be a failure unless we seek to discharge our obligations in the spirit of Jesus Christ." If that sounds like a pious platitude, we have only to call our own lives to the witness stand to refute it. Certainly the min-

[1] Hoyt, "The Preacher," p. 26.
[2] Forsyth, "Positive Preaching and the Modern Mind," p. 171.
[3] Lock, "St. Paul the Master-Builder," p. 69 f.
[4] "Ad Clerum," pp. 225–235.

istry is the last place in the world for a man who has been a failure elsewhere. There is no magic spell about the ministry to bring success to men who will not work with all their souls. "Fear God and work"[1] is a good motto for one who is a coworker with God in the highest of earth's callings.

2. *Appeal*

"We entreat also that ye receive not the grace of God in vain."[2] He is God's ambassador and it is really God's entreaty. "The entreaties of God" is Maclaren's expressive phrase.[3] If God can beseech man, surely God's ambassador should not be too haughty to plead with men. The word[4] here is difficult to translate. It has the triple meaning of entreaty, exhortation, and consolation. It is the chief function of the ambassador for Christ.[5] It is "as though God were entreating by us."[6] Paul has given his whole heart to the Corinthians. He has given them the real Gospel of Jesus. He is afraid that they will be tempted away from the simplicity and purity that is towards Christ.[7] But he cannot stand idly by and see the work in Corinth come to naught. They have received the grace of God. He begs that they do not render the very grace of God

[1] Broadus, "Sermons and Addresses," p. 347.
[2] 2 Cor. vi. 1.
[3] "Expositions of Holy Scripture," *in loco.*
[4] *Parakaloumen.*
[5] Stanley, *in loco.*
[6] 2 Cor. v. 20.
[7] 2 Cor. xi. 3.

of no avail, "in vain."[1] Paul does not pause to parley over the abstract question whether those who have the grace of God can make it null and void. He advises the Corinthians not to experiment with their eternal souls. He took no chances with himself.[2] He is in deadly earnest because the time is limited. It is always so with God's work. He hearkens and helps in the hour of opportunity, the acceptable[3] time. As it was in Isaiah's time[4] so it is now in the crisis in Corinth. As it was in Paul's day so is it to-day. Crisis is the word forever on the lips of the preacher and it must be so. "For there can be nothing worse, darker, arguing a nature more averse or indifferent to the highest good, than that God should plead, and I should steel my heart and deafen mine ear against His voice. The crown of a man's sin, because it is the disclosure of the secrets of his deepest heart as loving darkness rather than light, is turning away from the divine voice that woos us to love and to God."[5] The "clatter of the streets and the whirr of the spindles" drown the still small voice of God. The sound of the preacher's voice as God's spokesman becomes monotonous, displeasing, commonplace, even repulsive. Immersed in the cares of this world men come to resent as an impertinence

[1] *To emptiness.* [2] 1 Cor. ix. 27. [3] Cf. 2 Cor. vi. 1.
[4] Isa. xlix. 8. [5] Maclaren, "Expositions," *in loco.*

and an interference the effort of the minister of Christ to press home to an issue the claims of God upon the life. "The true return for ministerial devotedness is a life given to God."[1] When the minister's appeal bears the fruit of a redeemed life he has ample reward for rebuff and discouragement. But, if in the end it is only failure, he may at least have the satisfaction of duty done, if so be that is true. The preacher sows beside all waters. He cannot tell which will bear fruit, this or that. "He must first of all believe in human nature. He must have faith in the capacity of the average man. God alone knows the soul and the extent of its undiscovered resources. The preacher who builds his hope on brilliant people only is doomed to disappointment."[2] The force of the minister's character gives great weight to his appeal and is often the decisive factor. A feeble appeal from a feeble man is useless. "In any position, a vacillating man is feeble and unsatisfactory. But a vacillating leader is a positive calamity. The minister of the Gospel is the leader of his congregation, and for him to vacillate, in any great question, is practically to bring the army to a standstill, almost to proclaim the reign of anarchy."[3] At any rate the preacher must make the appeal in

[1] F. W. Robertson, "Life and Letters," etc., p. 661.
[2] Jefferson, "Building of the Church," p. 171.
[3] Blaikie, "The Work of the Ministry," p. 371.

behalf of Christ even if it fall upon deaf ears. One of the saddest phases of modern life is the large number of men in our cities who never go to church, who do not allow themselves to be troubled by the message of Christianity. There is, surely, a difference between Christianity and Churchianity.[1] Real disciples of Jesus are to be found outside of the churches. But it is still true that the churches are the main agencies for pushing the work of the kingdom of God.

3. *Giving No Occasion of Stumbling*

"Giving no occasion of stumbling in anything, that our ministration be not blamed."[2] Paul seems to think that some will actually be glad of an excuse not to listen to the message of the Gospel. They will be glad if the ministers of Christ give them such an excuse by glaring inconsistencies in their lives.[3] It is true that Paul's enemies in Corinth did not wait for an occasion. They manufactured numerous unfounded charges against Paul. They actually said that he knew that he was not a genuine apostle else he would have received pay for his services.[4] His very independent manhood was misunderstood and turned against him. But, none the less, Paul will

[1] Cf. Phelps, "Men and Books," p. 73.
[2] 2 Cor. vi. 3.
[3] Denney, *in loco.*
[4] 2 Cor. xi. 9 ff.

not change his conduct. He will cut off[1] occasion from those who are eager for an excuse to injure him and the cause of Christ. The beast is not far beneath the surface. Wolves jump on and devour the one in the pack who falls in the fight. It is true that men will find excuses anyhow for not accepting Christ as Saviour, but the minister must see to it that they have no real ground of complaint in his life, if it be possible to avoid it. No minister is perfect and, do the best one can, there will be occasion enough for stumbling[2] on the part of those always ready to cavil. Jesus felt very keenly the tragedy of men throwing stumbling-blocks in the way of those groping towards Him: "Woe unto the world because of occasions of stumbling, for it must needs be that the occasions come; but woe to that man through whom the occasion cometh."[3] And Mark[4] has it: "And whosoever shall cause one of these little ones that believe on Me to stumble, it were better for him if a great millstone were hanged about his neck, and he were cast into the sea." This peril is one common to all Christians, to all in fact, but it applies with peculiar force to ministers of the Gospel. The case of Judas Iscariot was in point. Paul will recall a sorrowful list of those who, like

[1] 2 Cor. xi. 12.
[2] Strike against.
[3] Matt. xviii. 7.
[4] Mark ix. 42.

Hymeneus and Alexander, have made shipwreck concerning the faith.[1] It is a sad business to dwell upon the careers of those who once stood forth as beacon lights of truth, whose light went out in darkness and even in disgrace. It cannot be justly objected if the press make a feature in the news columns of those ministers whose lives so fearfully belie their professions and their proclamations. It makes every lover of Christ wince with pain and hang his head in shame. But better far such public exposure of unfaithful preachers than concealment and secret distrust eating out the heart of love and confidence. After all the sober sense of the people may be counted on to see the difference and to rejoice all the more in the great body of the faithful soldiers of the Cross who with unostentatious piety go quietly and steadily forward in the work of Christ. Paul is conscious that he represents the honour of Christ before the world. He is determined that, if possible, no real ground of blame[2] shall attach to his ministry. The word[3] means blemish, blot, or disgrace. His desire is to keep his escutcheon clean, to wear an untarnished sword, to stoop to no tricks, to use no double-dealing, to live an open life before God and men. The tongues of the slanderers and tattlers will keep busy, beyond a doubt. He was particularly

[1] 1 Tim. i. 19 f. [2] 2 Cor. vi. 3. [3] *Momos.*

anxious to have clean hands in money matters and to do things honourable not only in the sight of God, but also in the sight of men.[1] Paul reveals thus a fine sense of business acumen and integrity. The minister cannot despise all the conventions of society merely because he is confident that God will understand his motives. The trouble is that people do not know all that God knows. The minister of Christ has no right to soil his reputation willfully or carelessly since his influence for Christ depends largely on his reputation. A man with a good character may lose his reputation and to a large extent his usefulness. Paul does not, of course, affirm that a minister who commits a sin can never be useful again. The case of Peter was too obvious a refutation of that idea. But, like other men, a minister who blights his reputation must build it up again. It is harder to rebuild than it is to build. Christ's look of pity on Peter had in it the elements of sympathy, compassion, and forgiveness, but Peter's heart was broken and he had to walk in the valley and the shadow and slowly climb out of the Slough of Despond. God can and does use the very faults of ministers for His glory, but there is no special call for us to commit an extra number in order to give the glory of God a fresh sphere of influence. We are

[1] 2 Cor. viii. 20 f.

not to sin in order that grace may abound. One of the keenest regrets of life is the thought that this or that unsaved soul might have been led to Christ but for the faults that he saw in us as men and ministers of Christ. So thus it behooves us all, as Paul[1] urged, to walk circumspectly.

Prof. G. A. Johnston Ross has a letter on the ministry in *The Yale News* in which he has very severe strictures on the present-day ministry. He is advocating the placing of young ministers for some years under the guidance of older ministers when the period of training in school is over. He laments the absence of this custom. "It is due to this more than to any other single fact that the ministry of the non-Episcopal churches is so largely filled with men of immeasurable pompousness and uncontrollable petulance. I honestly believe that it is in these and similar conditions that lies the origin of that something about the clerical character (including intellectual insincerity and personal unmanliness) which makes the clerical order so intolerably offensive to laymen." Dr. W. Robertson Nicoll makes a formal and very able protest against this indictment in *The British Weekly* for April 20, 1911. I must record my agreement with Dr. Nicoll so far as my own experience goes. There are bad men in every calling,

[1] Eph. v. 15.

but I have seen fewer in the ministry than anywhere else. I have taught some three thousand young ministers and the proportion of unmanly, insincere, ill-mannered, petulant men is very small in that number.

Prof. Johnston Ross has had a more unfortunate experience. The laymen as a rule greatly love the ministers in my opinion.

But Dr. Johnston Ross strikes a true note when he says: "The ministry is unmitigated misery for the man who may be described as constitutionally undevout; who is not what the Hebrews call 'a man of God'; his own relations with the ideal taking the form of interior colloquy—in other words, in some real sense he must be a man of prayer." This is finely said. Dr. Johnston Ross concludes his letter on "The Christian Ministry" with the warning "that no man should enter the ministry who can possibly keep out of it." That depends on what is meant. Certainly no one should enter the ministry without a strong sense of duty impelling him. But men can and do violate their sense of duty, refuse to hear the call of God or to heed when they hear. Jonah is not the only man who has run away from God's call. We do not, indeed, need a superfluity of ministers. If the laymen all did their full duty, fewer ministers would be required. But that is an ideal state still far ahead of us. At present the crying demand is for more men to man the churches and to push the work in mission fields at home and abroad. We do need the best men by nature, grace and equipment; but we also need more men, if the work is not to stagnate and decay. I quite agree with this word of Dr. Johnston Ross: "The times in the past when the land was overrun by ecclesiastics have been times of moral laxity and dissension." The fewer of such "ecclesiastics" the world has the better. God speed the exit of all of them. The work of Christ in the world calls for men of prophetic spirit and power, not priestly ecclesiastics who are professional parrots or tyrannical hypocrites. The Roman Catholic clergy of the middle ages is not the standard for the modern minister nor the type to which our world will give heed.

4. *Commending Ourselves as Ministers of God*

"But in everything commending ourselves as ministers of God."[1] The merely negative attitude is not enough, though one has a hard time just to keep from doing wrong. That of itself is a tremendous task. Exactly what Paul means is this: We commend ourselves as God's servants commend themselves.[2] The minister's letter of commendation to

[1] 2 Cor. vi. 4.

[2] Meyer, *in loco.*

his flock is his life. That is the one which they will read in preference to the sermon or to the Bible. The minister's life is an open book to his people and to the world. It is vain for him to bid men do as he says, not as he does. What Emerson so pithily said is literally true. What the preacher is thunders so loud into men's ears that they cannot hear what he says. This appeal to life is inevitable. The preacher must meet life as it is. And Paul is not afraid. These glowing verses [1] form a fit climax to Paul's sustained flight in praise of the Christian ministry. He has sought to interpret it according to its ideal and high purpose. He has placed it in bold contrast with the glory of the Mosaic dispensation. He has dared to look into the very Face of Christ. He has probed his own heart to the very bottom. He exposed the hearts of the men of his time. He is fully conscious that he has not fulfilled wholly the Ideal of the Christian minister. He makes no such claim for himself. But he is not willing to give up his ministry for any other calling in all the world. He has had his meed of suffering and sorrow, of disappointment and trial, of labour and anguish. He is willing to face all the facts of his ministry thus far and can still praise God with a full heart. He indulges in this spiritual dissection of his experiences

[1] 2 Cor. vi. 4–6.

as his closing contribution to the discussion of the ministry. After all it is not a matter of theory or romantic idea with Paul. He had his great experiences of the grace of God in Christ. No one can take them away from him. This richness of experience becomes the heritage of every servant of Christ. He can laugh at the doubts of tyros in religious matters. Many men with great names are novices in grace. The seasoned soldier of the Cross has been through the war with Christ. By the camp-fire of hallowed experiences they can renew the great hours when the Son of God walked in the fiery furnace with them. These men cannot be shaken by the attacks of all the infidels in the world. No amount of ignorance on the part of other men can make untrue the knowledge of Christ which they carry in their hearts. These triumphant spirits can enter fully into sympathy with Paul as he now reviews his life as a minister of God. There is a rhetorical device in Paul's grouping of his experiences. He divides them according to three words: *in*,[1] *by*,[2] *as*.[3] It is not wholly artificial as will be seen. The whole section is an expansion of "in everything."

(*a*) *Environment and Conduct.* Bernard[4] calls this division outward hardships and inward grace. This sharp contrast between environment and inward

[1] *En.* [2] *Dia.* [3] *Hos.* [4] *In loco.*

grace is manifest in the life of many another minister of Christ. Paul does not mean to claim any monopoly in such experiences as he here recounts. They are the common lot of men who go to the frontier for Christ. Missionaries in all ages can present detailed reproductions of what Paul here gives in no sense of boasting, but rather with humble gratitude for the goodness of God in it all. He is thus a "pattern" or sample preacher as he is a pattern sinner. It will be necessary to follow Paul's words rather minutely to catch the richness of feeling with which his heart is filled. "The fountains of the great deep are broken up within him as he thinks of what is at issue; he is in all straits, as he begins, and can speak only in disconnected words, one at a time; but before he stops he has won his liberty, and pours out his soul without restraint." [1] Paul's ministry at Corinth is challenged and hence he opens his heart as he would not otherwise do. But even so he is speaking not merely for himself, but for all ministers of Christ who shall meet a like crisis. His hardships had called for much patience.[2] Tribulation had wrought patience [3] in Paul. One may express a bit of surprise at this emphasis on patience in an epistle so full of turbulent emotion as is 2 Cor-

[1] Denney, *in loco.*
[2] Mentioned twice elsewhere in this Epistle, i. 6; xii. 12.
[3] Rom. v. 3.

inthians. But Paul's notion of patience is not silent acquiescence. The word[1] means remaining under. With all the vehement passion of a spirited horse Paul remains in the traces and thus shows patience. He has *Sturm und Drang*, but he holds himself in leash and keeps to his task. Indeed the grace of patience is called for in all this list of outward hardships in verses four and five. The "afflictions,"[2] "necessities," "distresses" are very general terms descriptive of his experiences. And yet they differ. The afflictions crush one like a heavy weight. The necessities[3] suggest loss of liberty and confinement. Distresses[4] reveal perplexity as in sickness,[5] loss of friends.[6] Hemmed in on every side he learned patiently to endure. Paul is now more particular. The "stripes"[7] he had received above measure,[8] a most humiliating experience for a proud spirit like Paul. The Jews had beaten him five times with forty stripes save one. That was the limit of the Mosaic law.[9] Sometimes death resulted from such scourging.[10] Thrice Paul was beaten with rods,[11] the Roman method of scourging. He had his "imprisonments"[12] also. They were "more abundant"[13]

[1] *Hypomone.*
[2] Cf. Rom. v. 1 f.; 2 Cor. xii. 10.
[3] Cf. 1 Cor. ix. 7.
[4] Cf. Rom. ii. 9; 2 Cor. xii. 10.
[5] 2 Cor. i. 6; xii. 7.
[6] 2 Tim. iv. 10; cf. Bernard, *in loco.*
[7] 2 Cor. xi. 23.
[8] 2 Cor. xi. 23.
[9] Deut. xxv. 3.
[10] Josephus, *Ant.*, 14, 8, 21.
[11] 2 Cor. xi. 25.
[12] Acts xvi. 24, etc.
[13] 2 Cor. xi. 23.

than the stripes. Up to this stage of Paul's life we are told in Acts of only one imprisonment [1] so that we must understand that the narrative in Acts is far from complete. The "tumults" [2] were also numerous and varied. His "labours" [3] were toils more exactly, with weariness and exhaustion of body and mind. They are even more abundant.[4] His "watchings" [5] were really "sleeplessnesses" and were "often." [6] He knew the nightmare of insomnia due to overwork and overanxiety, the nervous racking of mind and body in the slow-moving hours of night when he could find no rest. Paul's words read like the secret diary of many a minister of to-day. He had also "fastings" [7] not of a religious nature or for the sake of his health. Paul knew what it was to be "in hunger and thirst, in fastings often, in cold and nakedness." [8] The pangs of hunger, the pinch of poverty were no strangers to Paul,[9] the most gifted of all the ministers of Christ: "Even unto this present hour we both hunger, and thirst, and are naked, and are buffeted, and have no certain dwelling-place; and we toil, working with our own hands." This was not as it should have been even in that early

[1] Rom. xvi. 7. For further stripes see Acts xxii. 24.
[2] Cf. Acts xiii. 50; xiv. 5, 19; xvi. 22; xvii. 5; xviii. 12; xix. 29; xxi. 30.
[3] Cf. 2 Cor. xi. 27.
[4] 2 Cor. xi. 23.
[5] Cf. 2 Cor. xi. 27.
[6] 2 Cor. xi. 27.
[7] Cf. 2 Cor. xi. 27.
[8] 2 Cor. xi. 27.
[9] 1 Cor. iv. 11.

time of Christian origins. Paul commended the Philippians for their frequent thoughtfulness of his bodily needs.[1] After the lapse of the centuries the average minister of Jesus faces still the serious problem of actual living expenses. He must possess good business ability to be able to make both ends meet and keep out of debt, dress his family appropriately, educate his children, and lead his church in liberality. But Paul had no idea of giving up the ministry because of the shortcomings of the churches. He had his call from Jesus Christ. "Not that I speak in respect of want: for I have learned in whatsoever state I am, therein to be content."[2] That is a blessed secret when the preacher learns how to carry a high head with a hungry stomach, an upright look with an empty pocket, a happy heart with an unpaid salary, joy in God when men are faithless. It was just in the midst of such an untoward environment that Paul found that the graces of the heart grew like orchids on the wild rocks. These outward hardships proved to be the hot-bed for those flowers of the spirit. He is borne aloft and walks on the heights "in the Holy Spirit." This is the key to the list of graces in verses six and seven. Paul had found Jesus true to His word. The Holy Spirit was faithful to him in all these trials. By "pureness"[3]

[1] Phil. iv. 16. [2] Phil. iv. 11. [3] Cf. 2 Cor. vii. 11.

Paul means not only chastity, which is certainly included, but also purity of intention and thought, sincerity of motive.[1] By "knowledge"[2] he refers particularly to knowledge of divine things.[3] His very experiences gave him a keener perception of spiritual realities. Longsuffering[4] is a grace often attributed to God.[5] It is called for in an especial degree by a missionary like Paul.[6] Kindness[7] is also a divine attribute.[8] The love unfeigned,[9] like the other virtues, is due to the work of the Holy Spirit. Nothing but the new heart and the new view of man could make possible the deathless love for man which animated the heart of Paul. It was genuine and undying. The Word of truth[10] is a description of preaching. It is simple and unadulterated truth.[11] The Gospel deals with the eternal realities. The power of God[12] is just what Paul considers the Gospel itself to be, "the power of God unto salvation to every one that believeth."[13] The cross may be a stumbling-block to the Jews, and to the Greeks foolishness, but in reality it is both the power and the wisdom of God. These words of Paul are not mere random remarks. They are golden truths out of his

[1] Bernard, *in loco.* [2] *Gnosis.* [3] Cf. 1 Cor. xii. 8.
[4] Cf. 1 Tim. i. 16. [5] Rom. ii. 4; ix. 22, etc.
[6] Bernard, *in loco.* [7] Cf. Gal. v. 22.
[8] Rom. ii. 4; ix. 22, etc. [9] Cf. Rom. xii. 9.
[10] Cf. Eph. i. 13. [11] Stanley, *in loco.* Cf. 2 Cor. ii. 17.
[12] Cf. 2 Cor. xii. 9. [13] Rom. i. 16. Cf. 1 Cor. i. 18.

very heart. They characterize not merely Paul's vital apprehension of Christ, but express the joy and hope of every preacher of the Cross of Christ.

(*b*) *Mastery Over Circumstance.* "By the armour of righteousness on the right hand and on the left, by glory and dishonour, by evil report and good report."[1] There is progress in this group over the preceding one with "in." Here the use of "by" or "through"[2] suggests aggressive conflict rather than passive endurance of hardships with the spirit of resignation. There is the atmosphere of confidence, the swing of victory in these words. The use of the words "power of God" had already given a tonic to his words. Paul had already[3] elsewhere applied the figure of armour to the life of the Spirit. He had urged the Thessalonians to put on "the breastplate of faith and love; and for a helmet the hope of salvation." He will later, after long personal contact with the Roman soldier to whom he is chained, make a careful study of the Roman armour as illustrating the Christian conflict.[4] Here, however, it is only a passing allusion. He holds in his hands the weapons[5] of righteousness. Primarily, of course, this is the righteousness which is the gift of God, but there is also the other side of the truth, the actual

[1] 2 Cor. vi. 7 f. [2] *Dia.* [3] 1 Thess. v. 8.
[4] Eph. vi. 11 ff. [5] Cf. 2 Cor. x. 4.

righteousness of an upright life, the result of the grace of God in the life.[1] The conception is both offensive and defensive. The Christian minister, clad in Christ's righteousness, is ready for the battle. He can swing the sword of truth in his right hand and hold the shield of faith in his left. Nothing but this panoply of God can equip the soldier of Christ for the real war with the powers of evil in the world. No preacher can escape this battle save by compromise with his conscience. If he shut his eyes to the grip of the devil on the actual life of his community, the saloon, the gambling den, the brothel and other forces of corruption will let him alone. But, while the watchman sleeps upon the walls of Zion, young men and young women are swept on into the vortex of ruin. The white-slave traffic flourishes, the civic life is debauched, manhood is corrupted, the church becomes a respectable nonentity. If the preacher refuses to fight the actual evil in his community, he in a sense winks at that evil. If he does fight, the forces of evil will fight him. It is often with the preacher as it was with Nehemiah's men in building the walls of Jerusalem: "Every one with one of his hands wrought in the work, and with the other held his weapon."[2] Not every preacher has just this experience. There are idyllic pastures where the shep-

[1] Cf. Rom. vi.–viii.

[2] Neh. iv. 17.

herd leads his flock in peace and plenty.[1] But these havens of rest are growing fewer in the modern world. There is a drift away from many churches and the minister has to go out into the highways and hedges and compel them to come in. Those who used to come are now at week-end parties, on automobile rides, playing golf, or deep in the Sunday paper at home. It will not answer just to fuss and fret over the situation. The preacher must make it worth while for busy men and women to come to the worship of the sanctuary. He must be Wordsworth's "Happy Warrior":

> "Whose high endeavours are an inward light
> That makes the path before him always bright:
> Who, with a natural instinct to discern
> What knowledge can perform, is diligent to learn;
> Abides by this resolve, and stops not there,
> But makes his moral being his prime care;
> Who, doomed to go in company with pain,
> And fear, and bloodshed, miserable train!
> Turns his necessity to glorious gain;
> In face of these doth exercise a power
> Which is our human nature's highest dower.
>
> * * * * * * *
>
> But who, if he be called upon to face
> Some awful moment to which heaven has joined
> Great issues, good or bad for human kind,
> Is happy as a lover; and attired
> With sudden brightness, like a man inspired;
> And, through the heart of conflict, keeps the law
> In calmness made, and sees what he foresaw."

[1] Cf. Goldsmith's "Deserted Village."

The outcome may be "glory,"[1] or it may be "dishonour."[2] He is ready to pass through[3] the fire of criticism (dishonour) which his opponents are constantly kindling. It is useless for the preacher to be hyper-sensitive. He is not likely to suffer long from the woe because all men speak well of him. But often the excessive flattery of friends is even more perilous. But if one has a sense of integrity[4] (armour of righteousness), he can pursue the even tenor of his way. Some in Galatia would have plucked out their eyes for Paul. Others at Corinth thought he was out of his mind. Paul does not mean to say that he does not care. He does care very greatly. It stung his sensitive soul to the very quick. "Being reviled, we bless; being persecuted, we endure; being defamed, we entreat; we are made as the filth of the world, the offscouring of all things even until now."[5] He has become "a spectacle to the world, both to angels and men."[6] Each man must bear his own cross. This was a large part of Paul's crucifixion, the false imputations[7] of his conduct and motives which he met at every turn, among Jews, heathen, yea, and among the brethren. So he had learned how to take with outward complaisance "evil report" and "good report."[8] It was all in a day's journey. It was all a part of the

[1] 2 Cor. vi. 8. [2] 2 Cor. x. 2. [3] 2 Cor. xii. 14 ff.
[4] Denney, *in loco*. [5] 1 Cor. iv. 12 f. [6] 1 Cor. iv. 9.
[7] Stanley, *in loco*. [8] Cf. 1 Cor. iv. 13.

game of war with evil in which he was engaged. He was not disposed to complain of the conditions of service to Christ. Some personalities have more edge than others. Some men have more force and cut deeper into other lives. Some men cause more resistance to the Gospel than others who have the gift of persuasiveness. Christ takes us as we are and uses us with our varied gifts. Those in the "school of Christ" are "chosen by the Master to hear what He says, to see what He does, to learn what He is" and "are sent forth by the Master with a message, with a program, with a personality."[1] Much of human power in the ministry lies in personality. Paul was impossible to the Judaizing reactionaries. He is the inspiration of all lovers of spiritual truth and freedom in Christ.

(*c*) *Paradoxes in Paul's Ministry.* Antithesis runs through it all. Light and shadow interplay. The same cloud has its bright and its dark side. What is here true of Paul is true of every effective preacher of Christ. It was true of Jesus Himself. One can get a double report on almost any public man's life unless the man has been a nonentity. It is true that not all ministers of Christ have so much of tragedy as Paul experienced. The lives of most of us go on in a more commonplace manner.[2] But

[1] McDowell, "In the School of Christ," the Cole lectures for 1910.
[2] Denney, *in loco.*

there are men of heroic mould in the ministry who meet real crises with courage of heart whose fame is not blazoned abroad. Paul rises to a pæan of praise of the ministry. He began this wonderful "digression"[1] on the Christian ministry with an outburst of thanksgiving to God who always leads us in triumph in Christ.[2] He has soared with bold and steady wing till now with an eagle's sweep he swings a bit higher than before. He interprets to us his own secret heart in this last song before he comes down like the skylark. "As deceivers and yet true,"[3] he says. In the Clementine Homilies Paul is expressly termed "deceiver."[4] The Judaizers at Corinth had also applied this opprobious epithet to him. But Jesus Himself was charged with being a deceiver of the people.[5] Paul knew that he was true in heart and life, a teacher of truth, and was willing to let time give its final answer to the calumnies of his enemies. To-day the Judaizers are remembered chiefly because of their opposition to Paul who is the glory of the Roman world of his day. One needs the blind eye and the deaf ear[6] to much that comes before him. The preacher must have an intellectual culture that will command the respect of cultivated men and women, but it is far

[1] Stanley, *in loco*. [2] 2 Cor. ii. 12 f.
[3] So they had called Jesus "that deceiver" (Matt. xxvii. 63).
[4] Hom. II. 17, 18. [5] John vii. 12.
[6] Spurgeon, "Lectures to Students," Second Series, pp. 241 ff.

more important to have intellectual integrity.[1] He is a moral force primarily rather than an intellectual one. Paul is not here thinking so much about telling the truth in all of its aspects, though that is what one must do. It is being true that is in Paul's mind, a much deeper and more profound idea. At bottom a minister is an incarnation of truth and integrity. That is the reserve power in his character and work. Often the minister has to do his work with a pitifully slender apparatus [2] in the way of books and technical education. This is not to be endured if it can be remedied. But, if unavoidable, one can at least have a clean and open mind, glad to learn and loyal to all that is true and high. If one's manhood rings true, men will put up with a great deal in the preacher. If he slips a cog here, they will not endure him at all, however great gifts he may have.[3] Paul proceeds: "Unknown, and yet well known."[4] They accused Paul of being "obscure," not having right credentials, a nobody in the ministry, not recognized in high ecclesiastical circles.[5] According to this charge he was guilty of the crime of not being famous. Nobody cared what Paul thought or said. He could be ignored as one not in the company of the religious

[1] Phelps, "My Note-Book," p. 90.
[2] Spurgeon, "Lectures to Students," First Series, pp. 282 ff.
[3] Beecher, "Yale Lectures on Preaching," Third Series, p. 293.
[4] 2 Cor. vi. 9.
[5] Cf. 2 Cor. iii. 2; x. 10.

aristocrats. So the jibe ran. Paul easily retorts that he is "well known" among the true believers.[1] If he were as insignificant as his enemies claimed, they took a deal of trouble about him. There is a touch of irony here. What is fame after all? "As dying, and behold we live."[2] He seemed always on the point of death, but death kept vanishing into the distance. Doubtless his enemies had heard of his serious illness[3] at Corinth and were congratulating themselves that their troubles would soon be over with the providential death of Paul. But, lo, he comes back from the edge of the grave and is actually on his way to Corinth! It is amazing how virile some men of delicate constitution are. Paul lived to a fairly good old age and would have probably lived much longer but for his execution by Nero. He here makes merry over the anxiety of his enemies about his health. No minister has a right to trifle with his body. It is a holy temple for the indwelling of the Holy Spirit. The effectiveness of a minister is often marred or ruined by neglect or abuse of the body. Paul does not make light of the body in this raillery with his enemies. They simply need not count too certainly on his dying right away to oblige them. "As chastened, and not killed."[4] His enemies interpreted his troubles to

[1] Cf. 2 Cor. xi. 6. [2] 2 Cor. vi. 9. [3] 1 Cor. i. 9. [4] 2 Cor. vi. 9.

mean that God was afflicting him for his sins. Be it so. He is the last man to deny his need of the chastening rod. At any rate he is not yet killed. He can be thankful for that. Meanwhile he will endeavour to learn his lesson of chastisement which God may have for him. God can use these very enemies as a wholesome discipline for Paul. He will try to see that the lesson is not lost. There is banter in this play of words, but a note of utmost earnestness in it all. In these climacteric sentences Paul lets his imagination loose and it plays like lightning on the clouds. "As sorrowful, yet always rejoicing."[1] His opponents affect pity for Paul in his overmuch sorrow! This was only too true, however little Paul cared for their mock sympathy. He knew what sorrow was, but he was happy all the time. Laughter and tears lie close together in Paul's heart. The sorrow was a real note in his life, but it was interwoven with perpetual cheerfulness.[2] He had learned how to be anxious in nothing and to have the peace of God as the garrison for his heart.[3] So Chrysostom, the golden-mouthed preacher of Antioch and Constantinople, when banishment fell to his lot and out on the hot sands he sank down, could say: "Glory to God for all things." Paul, like Chrysos-

[1] 2 Cor. vi. 10.
[2] Cf. Rom. v. 3; Phil. iv. 4, 12.
[3] Phil. iv. 6 f.

tom, knew what it was to be a popular hero one day and the next to be taboo with the crowd. The preacher who tastes the sweets of popular applause is most likely to find some bitterness in the bottom of the cup before he has finished. "As poor, yet making many rich."[1] He was taunted by his enemies for not receiving pay for his work.[2] The word means literally a pauper. He had not entered the ministry to make money. He was entitled to support from the church at Corinth. He had refused to receive pay because he saw that he would be charged with having come after their money. Precisely this situation to-day confronts the missionaries in heathen lands, who must be supported by the home churches to remove this charge against them by the heathen. With Paul the case was much worse. The church at Jerusalem had taken apparently no interest in the missionary enterprise now that the apostles are themselves scattered over the world. The Judaizing element there threw every possible obstacle in Paul's path and misconstrued his motives and work to the brethren in Jerusalem.[3] The church at Antioch was a Greek church and heartily approved the missionary campaign of Paul, but, so far as any information is available, gave him no financial aid

[1] 2 Cor. vi. 10.
[2] 1 Cor. xi. 7; Phil. iv. 12.
[3] Cf. Acts xxi.

whatever. The "home" churches thus left Paul alone to do his work unaided. The older and more enlightened mission fields like Philippi did come to his relief at sporadic intervals. But in the main he was left to his own resources to do the most gigantic mission work of the ages in the teeth of the combined forces of Greek philosophy, Jewish prejudice, Roman antipathy, natural human depravity, and all the forces of sin and corruption in the greatest empire of the ancient world. He was poor, but he never had to beg. He was hungry, but he never starved. He worked with his own hands at his trade of tent-making and earned his bread. Thus he kept soul and body together so that he could preach the Gospel to a world that did not want to hear it and that was doing its utmost to thwart him in his efforts to evangelize the Roman Empire. A weak man would have quailed long before this. But Paul was a hero, if ever the world saw one. The ministry calls for men of the heroic spirit who can overcome difficulties. "And others had trial of mockings and scourgings, yea, moreover, of bonds and imprisonment: they were stoned, they were sawn asunder, they were tempted, they were slain with the sword: they went about in sheepskins, in goatskins; being destitute, afflicted, ill-treated (of whom the world was not worthy), wandering in deserts and mountains and caves and the holes of the earth."[1] This is the spirit of the martyrs and missionaries through all the ages who have carried the cross all over the world. They did it to make many rich with the riches of Christ Jesus. There is no riches like that in Christ. Paul's wealth consisted in the souls won to Christ and enriched in Him.[2] These had everything, for they had Christ and God.[3] Paul's last paradox about the preacher is the culmination, "as having nothing, and yet possessing all things."[4] He had nothing at all that would give him a place in Wall Street to-day. He had no bank account at Alexandria or Rome. He had no grain ships on the Mediterranean. It has been thought by some that Paul's father in Tarsus had some property which Paul may have inherited later. Be that as it may, he certainly has no earthly store at this juncture. He had missed making money, but had won the whole world. He had to the full[5] all that was worth having, all that was enduring. He is the richest man in all the world as he writes the last words of this matchless panegyric on the Christian ministry. He counts up his treasures and they outweigh all the sordid wealth of Corinth with its *nouveaux riches* and crass philosophy and material-

[1] Heb. xi. 36–38. [2] 1 Cor. i. 5. [3] 1 Cor. iii. 22.
[4] 2 Cor. vi. 10. So Jesus in His later ministry had not where to lay His head.
[5] *Katecho.*

istic commercialism. Paul had long ago made his choice. It was over twenty years ago that Jesus met him in the way and halted his steps. He made his decision then and he has not recanted since. He deliberately cast his life into the scale of the moral and spiritual values as against the worldly and the material. He had seen the heavenly vision and heard the call of Jesus to go far hence to the Gentiles. He is still running his race and there is wind in him yet. He has all, for he has Christ. And Christ has all of him. There is the spring of eternal youth in Paul. "I can do all things in Him that strengtheneth me."[1] There is work in Paul yet. He has sung his song about the preacher. He comes down from the mountain top with the face of Christ in his heart, down to the work in the valley. But he will put no veil over his face. He will keep on looking at the face of Jesus and telling of the light of the knowledge of the glory of God in the face of Christ to every one who lifts to Him a face sin-stained and shadowed. Some day Paul will look Jesus full in the face again. "For now we see in a mirror, darkly; but then face to face: now I know in part; but then shall I know fully even as also I was fully known."[2] Even before then he will feel sure of victory: "I have fought the good fight, I have finished the course, I have kept

[1] Phil. iv. 13.

[2] 1 Cor. xiii. 12.

the faith: henceforth there is laid up for me the crown of righteousness, which the Lord, the righteous judge, shall give me at that day; and not to me only, but also to all them that have loved His appearing."[1] "And they that be wise shall shine as the brightness of the firmament; and they that turn many to righteousness as the stars forever and ever."[2]

[1] 2 Tim. iv. 7 f. [2] Dan. xii. 3.

2